TWAYNE'S WORLD LEADERS SERIES

EDITOR OF THIS VOLUME

Samuel Smith, Ph. D.

John Locke

John Locke

John Locke

WILLIAM S. SAHAKIAN
Suffolk University

MABEL LEWIS SAHAKIAN
Northeastern University

TWAYNE PUBLISHERS
A DIVISION OF G. K. HALL & CO., BOSTON

Library of Congress Cataloging in Publication Data

Sahakian, William S
  John Locke.

  (Twayne's world leaders series)
  "Selected bibliography of Locke's writings on education": p. 137-40.
  Includes bibliographies and index.
  1. Locke, John, 1632-1704. 2. Education — Philosophy. 3. Locke, John, 1632-1704 — Bibliography.
  I. Sahakian, Mabel Lewis, joint author. II. Title.
  LB475.L7S23   370.1'092'4   74-20735
  ISBN 0-8057-3539-9

DEDICATED TO JAMES N. SAMPLE
EDUCATOR AND FRIEND

Contents

About the Authors

Dr. Mabel Lewis Sahakian, currently Lecturer in Philosophy at Northeastern University where she has taught since the early 1960's, pursued her Ph.D. in the field of philosophy at Boston University. For almost a decade she has coauthored books with her husband William S. Sahakian. A popular lecturer at civic and church groups, as well as at universities, she has been singled out for a number of honors, including the *World Who's Who of Women; Who's Who of American Women; Contemporary Authors; Two Thousand Women of Achievement;* and *Dictionary of International Biography.* She has been a member of the Boston Authors Club and the American Philosophical Association. She is the coauthor with W. S. Sahakian of *Realms of Philosophy* (1965), *Ideas of the Great Philosophers* (1966) and *Rousseau as Educator* (Twayne Publishers, Inc., 1974).

William S. Sahakian undertook his graduate studies at Harvard and Boston Universities, receiving his Ph.D. from the latter institution. He is currently Professor of Philosophy and Psychology at Suffolk University. Dr. Sahakian has contributed to professional journals throughout the world, and his books include *History of Philosophy* (1968); *Ethics: Theories and Problems* (1974); *History of Psychology* (1968); and *Psychology of Personality* (rev. ed., 1974). He has written articles for the *Encyclopaedia Britannica* and the *International Encyclopedia of Psychiatry, Psychoanalysis, and Psychology.* His past and present professional affiliations include membership in the American Philosophical Association, the American Psychological Association, the New York Academy of Science, and Fellow of the Massachusetts Psychological Association. He has been selected for inclusion in *Who's Who in the World; Who's Who in America; Contemporary Authors; American Men of Science;* and the *International Scholars Directory.*

Preface

The paucity of books on Locke's philosophy of education is sufficient
warrant for this volume. The most useful book in print (*John Locke
and Education* by John W. Yolton) does not treat adequately all the
various educational writings of Locke but limits itself chiefly to his
classic, *Some Thoughts concerning Education*. Another helpful
volume is James L. Axtell's book of readings: *The Educational
Writings of John Locke*. Axtell's book draws on most of the primary
sources but omits some valuable material, however, such as those
portions of Locke's *An Essay concerning Human Understanding*
that deal with philosophical concepts important for an appreciation
of Lockean educational theory.

Without an understanding of Locke's basic philosophy, especially
his epistemology (theory of knowledge) and, interrelated thereto his
metaphysics (theory of ultimate reality), it would be difficult to
grasp his philosophy of education. In fact, even more is required: an
understanding of his ethical theories and philosophy of religion. In
this volume all these aspects are discussed in considerable detail.
Also included are the following special features which provide con-
venient quick-reference information: (1) a chronology of events
related to the life, writings, and educational philosophy of Locke; (2)
a chart showing the chronological relationships between Locke and
other great philosophers and educators; and (3) two annotated bibliographies.

WILLIAM S. SAHAKIAN
MABEL LEWIS SAHAKIAN

Boston, Massachusetts

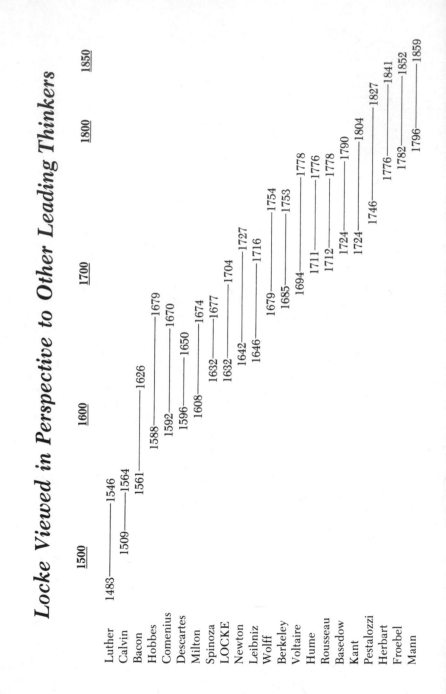

Locke Viewed in Perspective to Other Leading Thinkers

Chronology

1606   Birth of Locke's father, John Locke, Sr., on April 29.
1630   Marriage of Locke's father to his mother, Agnes (or Anne) Keene on July 15.
1632   Birth of Locke at Wrington, Somerset County, England, on August 29.
1637   Baptism of Locke's younger brother Thomas, who was born at Belluton.
1646 - School years at Westminster School.
1652
1651   Birth of Edward Clarke of Chipley.
1652 - Undergraduate years at Christ Church, Oxford University.
1655
1654   First publication (some verses while a student at Oxford).
1656   Bachelor's degree.
1660   Appointment as tutor at Christ Church, Oxford University.
1661   Death of Locke's father.
1663   Publication of *Essays on the Laws of Nature*. Death of Locke's brother Thomas.
1665   Departure for Cleves as secretary to Sir Walter Vane, Elector of Brandenburg.
1666   Return to Oxford and study of medicine. Successful therapy for Lord Ashley, later Earl of Shaftesbury (Lord High Chancellor of England in 1672).
1667   Matriculation of Locke's friend Edward Clarke at Wadham College, Oxford.
1667 - Residence with Lord Ashley.
1675
1668   Election as a Fellow of the Royal Society.
1670 - First drafts of *An Essay concerning Human Understanding*.
1671
1672   Appointment as Secretary for the Presentation of Benefices.

1673 Promotion to the Secretaryship of the Board of Trade.

1675 Marriage of Edward Clarke of Chipley and Mary Jepp of Sutton Court. Termination of Shaftesbury's position as chancellor.

1675 - Sojourn in France, driven by illness to Montpellier and Paris.
1679

1676 - Shaftesbury committed to the Tower of London.
1677

1677 Association in Montpellier with Thomas Herbert, Earl of Pembroke, to whom *An Essay concerning Human Understanding* was dedicated in 1690.

1677 - Service as tutor to the son of Sir John Banks (in France).
1679

1678 Residence in Paris. Association in Paris with the scientist Nicholas Thoynard and the physician Dr. Peter Guenellon of Amsterdam. Visit to Bordeaux and Lyons.

1679 Return to London and Lord Shaftesbury. Assistance in the education of Lord Shaftesbury's grandson. Shaftesbury's appointment as president of the Privy Council. Return to Oxford in December (in student quarters) after absence of 4½ years.

1680 Return to London at Thanet House as Shaftesbury's physician and political advisor.

1681 Visit with James Tyrell at Oakley in Buckinghamshire. Residence at Oxford for a year and a half with occasional London visits. Shaftesbury's second arrest and confinement in the Tower of London; released later the same year.

1681 - Literary tasks in his student quarters at Oxford.
1682

1682 Escape of Shaftesbury to Amsterdam on November 25.

1683 Death of Shaftesbury in Amsterdam on January 28.

1683 - Exile in Holland.
1689

1684 Loss of his Oxford studentship. First of the letters to Clarke written on July 19. Three-month tour through the provinces of the Netherlands.

1685 His extradition from Holland demanded on May 7. Clarke taken into custody for his "correspondence with traitors."

1686 Contacts with the Genevese, Jean Le Clerc, editor of *Bibliothèque Universelle et Historique*. Publication in French of *Method of Indexing a Commonplace Book*.

Chronology

1687   Departure from Amsterdam for residence in Rotterdam.

1687 - Publication of the abstract of *An Essay concerning Human*
1688   *Understanding* in Le Clerc's *Bibliothèque Universelle.*

1688   Arrival of Clarke, with his wife and daughter, in Holland. Departure of William of Orange for England.

1689   Publication of *A Letter concerning Toleration*. Return to England.

1690   Publication of *A Second Letter concerning Toleration*. Publication of *Two Treatises on Government*. Publication of *An Essay concerning Human Understanding*. Completion of manuscript for *Some Thoughts concerning Education*.

1691   Residence with Sir Francis and Lady Masham at Oates.

1692   Publication of *A Third Letter concerning Toleration*. Publication of *Some Considerations of the Consequences of the Lowering of Interest and the Raising of the Value of Money.*

1693   Publication of *Some Thoughts concerning Education.*

1694   Establishment of Bank of England by an Act of Parliament with Locke as an original proprietor.

1695   First of a series of epistles addressed to a political club (the "College") to influence Parliament. Publication of *Short Observations on a Printed Paper entitled, "For Encouraging the Coining of Silver Money in England, and After for Keeping it Here."* Publication of *The Reasonableness of Christianity, as Delivered in the Scriptures.* Publication of *A Vindication of the Reasonableness of Christianity from Mr. Edward's Reflections.*

1696 - Appointment (May 15, 1696) as a salaried commissioner on
1700   the Council of Trade and Plantations.

1699   Publication of fourth edition of *An Essay concerning Human Understanding* (last edition during Locke's lifetime).

1703   Manuscript of *Some Thoughts concerning Reading and Study for a Gentleman.*

1704   Death of Locke (October 28). Inheritance of Locke's estate by Peter King (Locke's cousin) and Frank Masham (son of Sir Francis and Lady Masham).

1705 - Publication of *Paraphrases on the Epistles of St. Paul.*
1707

1706   Publication of *A Fourth Letter concerning Toleration.*

1714   Publication of *Works of John Locke* (in 3 vols.).

CHAPTER 1

Locke: A Biographical Perspective

T HAT monumental intellectual figure John Locke, whose *An
Essay concerning Human Understanding* (published in 1690)
is credited with opening the period of the Enlightenment, was born
in Wrington, Somerset on August 29, 1632. He was born less than a
century after the two greatest English philosophers of the
Renaissance: seventy-one years after Francis Bacon (1561 - 1626),
forty-four years after Thomas Hobbes (1588 - 1679). He was senior
by ten years to Sir Issac Newton (1642 - 1727). Among other famed
contemporaries were three of the leading rationalist philosophers of
Europe, with whom he engaged in considerable discussion and
debate, namely, René Descartes (1596 - 1650), Benedict Spinoza
(1632 - 1677), and Gottfried Wilhelm Leibniz (1646 - 1716); thus, he
was thirty-six years younger than Descartes, the same age as
Spinoza, and fourteen years older than Leibniz.
  When Locke died on October 28, 1704, Immanuel Kant (1724 -
1804), whose classic *Critique of Pure Reason* (published in 1781)
marked the close of the period of the Enlightenment, was not yet
born. The famous French writer and deist Voltaire (1694 - 1778),
who did much to disseminate the ideas of the Enlightenment
throughout France and on the Continent, was only ten. Of the two
eminent British philosophers who were to continue developing
Locke's philosophy of empiricism — the Irish philosopher George
Berkeley (1685 - 1753) and the Scottish philosopher David Hume
(1711 - 1776) — the former was twenty and the latter not yet born.
  Wrington, the birthplace of Locke, is one of many charming towns
in rural England. It is vividly portrayed by Benjamin Rand:

Under the shadow of the Mendip Hills, in the county of Somerset in
England, in a pleasant and fruitful vale, nestles the old market town of
Wrington. With numerous thatched houses, often irregularly built, it is in

appearance not unlike many other ancient English villages, but it gains a certain degree of outward distinction from its parish church, a stately edifice with a tower that has been described as one of the most beautiful in the kingdom. More important far, however, is the fame it has attained from the fact that in an old thatched cottage adjoining the grounds of the church was born on the 29th of August, 1632, the philosopher John Locke. The parents of Locke belonged to the Somerset village of Belluton, but his birth occurred while his mother was on a visit to her brother at Wrington.[1]

It was in the country atmosphere of Belluton that Locke spent the first fourteen years of his life before leaving to attend school at Westminister.

I *Childhood Years*

Locke was named after his father, John Locke, who was educated in law and became a country attorney as well as clerk to the justices of the peace in Somersetshire. The elder Locke sided with the Parliamentarians rather than with the Royalists, although the West was dominated by the latter. When the Civil War erupted between King Charles I and the Long Parliament, he served as a captain in the Parliamentary army; as a consequence he suffered considerable financial losses. However, the monetary legacy Locke received from his father was to stand him in good stead for many years to come.

Locke's mother, a decade older than her husband and thirty-five years of age when Locke was born, is remembered as a "very pious woman and affectionate mother." She died when Locke was twenty-two.

Locke, the elder of two brothers, was quite distant from his father until later in life when he reached his maturity. The father saw that the two boys acquired a fine education, but the younger brother died early. Locke, reared in the strictest discipline that a Puritan home could provide, knew his father as a severe disciplinarian until his adult years when signs of warm feelings were detectable. Having been tutored early in the significance of political liberty, Locke listened to his father's expositions on the people's right to sovereignty as represented by their chosen Parliament through free elections. Notwithstanding the fact that Locke's later views were altered and expanded, his basic *Weltanschauung* was permanently fixed as a child in his father's home.

Severe and strict as his father was during Locke's childhood years, the father's discipline must have had a salutary effect on the young

Locke because he later expressed his indebtedness to his father's wholesome influences during his boyhood years, and later incorporated them into his principal work on the philosophy of education, *Some Thoughts concerning Education.* Apparently Locke approved of his father's training tactics and of his pedagogical technique.

From Mr. Locke I have often heard of his father, that he was a man of parts. Mr. Locke never mentioned him but with great respect and affection. His father used a conduct towards him when young that he often spoke of afterwards with great approbation. It was the being severe to him by keeping him in much awe and at a distance when he was a boy, but relaxing, still by degrees, of that severity as he grew up to be a man, till, he being become capable of it, he lived perfectly with him as a friend. And I remember he has told me that his father, after he was a man, solemnly asked his pardon for having struck him once in a passion when he was a boy.[2]

Severity of rearing must not be construed as cruelty. Philosophizing later with respect to his early training, Locke commented: "Those that intend ever to govern their children should begin it whilst they are *very little*, and look that they perfectly comply with the will of their parents."[3] He added:

Would you have your son obedient to you when past a child; be sure then to establish the authority of a father *as soon* as he is capable of submission, and can understand in whose power he is. If you would have him stand in awe of you, imprint it in his *infancy;* and as he approaches more to a man, admit him nearer to your familiarity; so shall you have him your obedient subject (as is fit) whilst he is a child, and your affectionate friend when he is a man. For methinks they mightily misplace the treatment due to their children, who are indulgent and familiar when they are little, but severe to them, and keep them at a distance, when they are grown up. For liberty and indulgence can do no good to *children;* their want of judgment makes them stand in need of restraint and discipline, and on the contrary, imperiousness and severity is but an ill way of treating men, who have reason of their own to guide them; unless you have a mind to make your children, when grown up, weary of you, and secretly to say within themselves, *When will you die, father?*[4]

II   *Attendance At Westminster School*

At the age of fourteen, in 1646, Locke matriculated at Westminster School. Admission into this distinguished school was quite difficult, requiring the recommendation of men of influence sponsoring promising youths of their own party. The school, which had been heretofore the domain of Loyalists exclusively, began admitting the sons of Puritans. It was Colonel Alexander Popham, a member of Parliament and friend of Locke's father, who nominated the youth to Westminster.

The six years Locke spent at Westminster School were devoted largely to Greek and Latin studies, a pedagogical methodology that he subsequently regarded with disapproval. Later (in 1691) he wrote of the school to his friend Clarke regarding the latter's son:

I am satisfied about your son that he wants not parts, so that if he has not made all the progress we could have desired I lay it wholly upon want of application, which I guess is owing something to a saunteringness that is in his temper. . . . I think he is better reconciled to his book, for he comes sometimes of himself to me to show me what he hath done and to ask what he shall do next; though he has not all the alacrity towards it I could wish, and I know not whether there be some cunning in it for fear I should represent matters so to you, that I should incline you to send him to Westminster School, of which and the discipline used there I have given him such a representation that I imagine he has no great liking to it.

I might advise you to Westminster, or some other very severe school, where if he were whipped soundly whilst you are looking out another fit tutor for him, he would perhaps be the more pliant and willing to learn at home afterwards.[5]

Charles I was beheaded in 1649, three years after Locke entered Westminster School, but it is doubtful that Locke witnessed that dreadful sight inasmuch as his headmaster, Richard Busby, vehemently opposed Cromwell.

Westminster School was in operation about a century before Locke arrived at the institution, which had been chartered by Henry VIII. Henry's plan called for forty boys, but the school's reorganization under Queen Elizabeth provided for eighty boys in addition to the forty King's scholars, or foundationers. Of the eighty, some of the boys resided with masters of the school and were known as *pensionarii;* others were *oppidani,* or town boys, who lived with their own parents or relatives. At the conclusion of four years, six students chosen for their academic acumen were provided with tuition-free scholarships and expenses to attend Christ Church, Oxford University, and Trinity College, Cambridge University, for seven years, three students to each university. Christ Church College is Oxford University's most prestigious, and Trinity College has the same status at the University of Cambridge. By the time of Locke's admission to Westminster School, there were more than eighty boys in addition to the forty King's scholars, and within a year he was made a King's scholar (1647). Requirements in order to become a *peregrinus* (country boy boarding with one of the school's neighbors, as Locke was) included a rudimentary knowledge, fine moral stature, and a mind capable of being educated. To be elevated to the rank of King's scholar required passing a rigorous examination in Greek and Latin, writing ability, and knowledge of "at least eight parts of grammar." When a boy achieved this level, both tuition and residency fees were suspended, and an annual allowance was granted.

After six academic years at Westminster School, Locke left in 1652 as a King's scholar to enter Christ Church, Oxford University, having obtained a junior studentship.

III *Studies at Oxford University*

In the fall of 1652 Locke was admitted to the University of Oxford; the *Christ Church College Entry Book* contained the descriptive entry appended to his name: *generosi filius* ("son of a gentleman"). When Locke's junior studentship terminated in 1659, he was elected to a senior studentship, permitting him to remain permanently with the university, for it carried a life tenure. Before long he was a lecturer in Greek and rhetoric; and by 1661 he had been appointed censor (students' supervisor or advisor) in moral philosophy, notwithstanding the fact that such appointments were normally granted only to the clergy.

Locke entered Oxford when the Royalists had reached the end of their era. Oliver Cromwell came as chancellor, and Puritans sought to purge Oxford of the remaining Royalists, or "malignants," as they called them. All but three of the college heads lost their position. By 1650 prosperity and a normal academic life had returned, and a nucleus of the Royal Society had been organized. In his *Oxford in the Age of John Locke,* Hargreaves-Mawdsley depicted it as follows:

When therefore in 1652 John Locke entered Christ Church, it was into a University community which, fast recovering, contained within it men famous in philosophy and the sciences: Thomas Sydenham, the physician; Jonathan Goddard, the first Englishman to make a telescope; John Wallis, who had worsted Hobbes in philosophical controversy; and a wealthy visitor from London, Robert Boyle. Christopher Wren (1632 - 1723), although the same age as Locke, had already graduated and was an All Souls fellow.[6]

Locke's Oxford was a city walled and gated, with its gardens, muddy, unpaved streets, fields, and nearby rivers. It was a city of taverns and of bells where the cry of the watchman could be heard during the night. Academic caps and gowns were worn everywhere. It was a period of the blossoming of natural philosophy. Arts and sciences mingled as did "moral" philosophers with the "natural" philosophers, the two in close association in the Royal Society. The academic atmosphere was permeated with optimism and expectancy. Christ Church, Locke's college, was the theological center, holding the new Oxford attitude in suspicion. An isolated city, Oxford was quite removed from the other cities of England. The coach consumed thirteen hours traveling from Oxford to London in summer, and two days in winter, whereas today it is a question of approximately an hour by train. A coach from Oxford to Bath, Reading, or Birmingham in 1707 made the trip only once every two weeks, to Shrewsbury once a month, to Exeter once in five weeks, and to Westmorland a mere three times a year.

Unlike the university buildings in the United States, which have been replaced by new construction, those of Oxford University when Locke attended still stand and are in use, with the stone steps to upper floors heavily worn from constant use throughout the centuries. The Oxford of Locke's time is still very much in evidence in these ancient buildings, some of which date from the thirteenth century.

In Locke's Oxford, there was a small library of books and manuscripts housed by Sir Thomas Bodley (the Bodleian Library came into existence in 1598), but there was no scientific laboratory until the Ashmolean Laboratory of chemistry was built in 1683 (named after Elias Ashmole). The laboratory became the center for Oxford science, and the radiation of Oxford science extended beyond England to continental Europe.

Locke was twenty years old when he arrived as an undergraduate at Oxford. What was his life like there? Students arose each morning by five in order to attend chapel, where the Westminster Assembly controlled the liturgy, displacing that of the Church of England. After church there was breakfast followed by classes until midday dinner (during meals Latin was the only language permitted), after which followed another compulsory lecture. This schedule was interrupted with a four o'clock sermon at Christ Church on Thursdays and preparations for Sabbath devotions on Saturday afternoons. University Acts, oral examinations taken by those pursuing the bachelor of arts degree, were also held in the afternoons. (Locke found these University Acts quite irritating.) Vesper services were conducted daily at the college's chapel, Christ Church Cathedral, after which Locke would go to his tutor's study along with his undergraduate colleagues, where he heard prayers and rendered an account of his day's activities. The time was his own after this; if he did not go for a walk (provided he had his tutor's permission), he would relax or retire, for bedtime came early.

The first-year curriculum at Oxford in Locke's time included rhetoric (Monday and Thursday mornings) and grammar (Tuesday and Friday mornings). The second-year curriculum called for logic, taught by a fellow of Christ's College (Monday and Thursday mornings), and moral-philosophy lectures, delivered by an appropriate professor (Tuesday and Friday mornings). Logic continued in the third year (Monday and Thursday) as did moral philosophy (Tuesday and Friday), but geometry (Wednesday and Saturday mornings) and Greek (Wednesday and Saturday afternoons) were added. The eight-lecture week followed through to the fourth and final year of college, during which, in addition to the same courses taken during the junior year, the students participated in public debates in Latin. In the first year or two at the college, they worked independently, subject to some tutorial supervision, studying Latin, Greek, Hebrew, and other subjects considered elementary.

These insipid courses that Locke was forced to endure while at Oxford were far from his liking, but he had to suffer them until his graduation on February 14, 1656, when the A.B. degree was conferred on him. When Locke wrote his *Some Thoughts concerning Education* in 1693, he seized the opportunity to strike back at the Oxford curriculum by commenting:

Rhetoric and logic being the arts that in the ordinary method usually follow immediately after grammar, it may perhaps be wondered that I have said so little of them. The reason is, because of the little advantage young people receive by them; for I have seldom or never observed anyone to get the skill of reasoning well, or speaking handsomely, by studying those rules which pretend to teach it: And therefore I would have a young gentleman take a view of them in the shortest systems [that] could be found, without dwelling long on the contemplation and study of those formalities. Right reasoning is founded on something else than the *predicaments* and *predicables*, and does not consist in talking in *mode* and *figure* itself.[7]

Locke is here attacking the course in logic at Oxford which one scholar termed a "debased Aristotelianism." Rather than finding satisfaction with his Oxford studies, Locke sensed exasperation and felt that they brought little light to his understanding.

The only philosophy taught at Oxford was Aristotelianism, but Locke's appreciation of the French philosopher Descartes and rationalism derives from his tutor at Oxford, who was a Cartesian. Locke's positive response to geometry stems from his junior year at college, when he studied under John Wallis, whose rendition of geometry extended to logic, mechanics, and music! With Wallis in mind, Locke wrote:

Arithmetic is the easiest, and consequently the first sort of abstract reasoning, which the mind commonly bears or accustoms itself to: And is of so general use in all parts of life and business, that scarce anything is to be done without it. This is certain, a man cannot have too much of it, nor too perfectly.[8]

Thus Locke, like the French rationalist philosopher Descartes, was enamored of mathematics. Locke was also philosophically indebted to his countryman Francis Bacon, but he regarded Bacon's efforts as no more than pioneering. Cartesian rationalism was stimulating and refreshing to Locke, in contrast to the only type of philosophy then being taught at Oxford, which he dismissed as an almost entirely wasteful effort, an Aristotelianism "perplexed with obscure terms and useless questions." The rationalism of Spinoza, despite its consistency with Cartesianism, and notwithstanding the fact that Locke was Spinoza's contemporary (Locke the senior by only three months), seems to have been without influence upon Locke.

It was the approach of Descartes that Locke adopted, a method of skepticism that repudiated prevailing dogmas and other influences. Descartes had turned within himself to find truth. The Cartesian dictum *Cogito, ergo sum* ("I think, therefore I am"), postulating the certain consciousness of one's own existence, the awareness of one's own consciousness, was for Descartes the only basis on which to found a philosophy issuing in certitude. Fundamental Cartesian theses were consciousness as the basis of certainty and deduction as the method of certainty.

Weary of Aristotelianism and the mystifying character of scholasticism, Locke, pleased with the start afforded by Descartes, began constructing his empiricist philosophy on the basis of what he found in consciousness, in experience. (For Locke, knowledge involves two kinds of ideas: simple or elementary ideas derived from experiences or reflection about them, and complex ideas created by our minds as they abstract, compare, and combine the simple elementary ideas. True knowledge discloses the relationships between ideas and reality.) However, Locke was not blind to the shortcomings of Descartes, for he carefully evaluated the Cartesian doctrine of innate ideas — the doctrine that man is born with clear and undeniably true ideas — found it wanting, and repudiated it before assuming his own antithetical empirical stance.

After obtaining his A.B. degree in 1656, Locke went in pursuit of his A.M., which was conferred on him in June, 1658. It was shortly after this time that he was elected to a senior studentship (i.e., a fellowship) at Christ Church. Although he continued to study metaphysics, logic, moral philosophy, and natural philosophy (i.e., physics), he began to study subjects more to his liking, such as history. His delight in history was echoed in his *Some Thoughts concerning Education* when he remarked:

As nothing teaches, so nothing delights more than history. The first of these recommends it to the study of grown men, the latter makes me think it the fittest for a young lad, who as soon as he is instructed in chronology, and acquainted with the several *epochs* in use in this part of the world, and can reduce them to the *Julian Period,* should then have some *Latin History* put into his hand. The choice should be directed by the easiness of the style; for wherever he begins, chronology will keep it from confusion; and the pleasantness of the subject inviting him to read, the language will insensibly be got without that terrible vexation and uneasiness which children suffer where they are put into books beyond their capacity.[9]

Study for his master's degree also brought Locke under the influence of Lewis du Moulin, Professor of Ancient History, and Bishop Seth Ward, the first important Oxford astronomer, whose tenure ran from 1649 to 1661. Unlike his contemporary at the University of Cambridge, Sir Isaac Newton, Locke did not become a physicist or scientist. Despite his seeming aversion for Oriental languages, he was required to study Arabic and upgrade his knowledge of Hebrew toward fulfilling his requirements for the master of arts degree. In addition to the influence of du Moulin and Ward, Locke was also deeply influenced by Edward Pococke (1604 - 1691), Professor of Arabic and later of Hebrew.

Locke's task at Oxford was not burdensome; as a tutor he had ten or fewer students at any given time. Later, other duties came his way, including those (already mentioned) of lecturer in Greek and rhetoric and censor in moral philosophy.

IV *Early Career*

Locke's first appearance in print came in his twenty-second year, when he was invited to contribute to an Oxford anthology of poems in honor of Cromwell after the English victory in the war against the Dutch.[10] In the fall of the same year, 1654, his mother became ill while visiting relatives at Wrington and died on October 4 at the age of fifty-seven in the little cottage where Locke was born. His father, who had become seriously ill in the year of the Restoration (1660), died on February 13, 1661,[11] at the age of fifty-four. His brother Thomas died in 1663, leaving the philosopher quite alone.

In September, 1665, during the great plague of London, King Charles II and his court returned to Christ Church, Oxford (the previous visit having been in September, 1663). Soon afterward, in November, 1665, Locke left England for the post of secretary to the diplomatic mission of Sir Walter Vane to Brandenburg, a sensitive appointment since the embassy was of considerable importance to British policy because of the Dutch war.

Returning to Oxford in 1666, Locke broke with tradition by choosing medicine over holy orders. He met and began to collaborate with Thomas Syndenham, the famous English physician. He also became acquainted with Lord Ashley (Anthony Ashley Cooper), later Earl of Shaftesbury and Lord High Chancellor of England, whom he treated and cured, with whom he resided in London (1667 - 1675) and shared liberal ideas in favor of civic and intellectual liberty and on whose life he was to exercise considerable influence. Locke received a Bachelor of Medicine degree in 1674.

On November 23, 1668, at the age of thirty-six, Locke was elected a Fellow of the Royal Society. His sponsor, Sir Paul Neile, was a friend of Lord Ashley. When the latter had been appointed to the post of Chancellor of the Exchequer (1661), Locke became interested in economics. In order to achieve economic progress, Locke felt it necessary to overcome the deep-seated belief that usury was wrong. When usury was legalized in 1546, the government imposed a legal limit of 10 percent, later reduced to 6 percent in 1651. Sir Josiah Child advocated a further reduction to 4 percent as enforced successfully in Holland. Locke, replying to Child in a 1668 manuscript, argued that the first thing to be considered is whether the price of the hire of money can be regulated by law; and to that, I think, generally speaking that 'tis manifest it cannot. For, since it is impossible to make a law that shall hinder a man from giving away his money or estate to whom he pleases, it will be impossible by any contrivance of law, to hinder men . . . to purchase money to be lent to them at what rate soever their occasions shall make necessary for them to have it.[12]

Locke held that money, comparable to any commodity, fluctuated at its own market rate. Not the law, but the market rate should govern the rate of interest.

Money has a value as it is capable by exchange to procure us the necessaries and conveniences of life, and in this it has the nature of a commodity; only with this difference that it serves us commonly by its exchange, never almost by its consumption.[13]

Important in Locke's spiritual development was Benjamin Whichcote, the leading Latitudinarian divine of the Cambridge School, who was inducted as vicar of St. Laurence Jewry in the city of London, and of whose congregation Locke became a member. (Latitudinarianism, the product of rational theology, was originally an Oxford movement.)

By January of 1669 Locke had already begun to suffer seriously from asthma, a disease that was to torment him for the remainder of his life. Although the final draft of his *An Essay concerning Human Understanding* (1690) was not written until the late 1680s, two drafts were made in 1671. It was in 1672 that the King gave Shaftesbury the post of Lord High Chancellor of England, the most coveted and powerful ministerial office in the realm. Locke in consequence was appointed Secretary of Presentations, a somewhat obscure post, but on October 15, 1673, Locke became secretary of the Council of Trade and Plantations, he himself being one of the merchant adventurers.

V.   *Travels in France*

Locke sojourned in France from 1675 to 1679, ostensibly for reasons of health. Coincidentally the Whigs, to which party Locke belonged, entered into secret negotiations with the French court with the objective of removing the king's new chief minister, the Earl of Danby, from power. This goal having been accomplished,

Locke returned immediately to England. Meanwhile Shaftesbury, formerly a member of the king's cabal of advisors, who had become head of the Whig opposition and a severe critic of the king's policies, was committed to the Tower. In a letter written in 1704, Shaftesbury's grandson wrote:

When my grandfather quitted the Court and began to be in danger from it, Mr. Locke now shared with him in dangers as before in honours and advantages. He entrusted him with his secretest negotiations, and made use of his assistant pen in matters that nearly concerned the State and were fit to be made public to raise that spirit in the nation which was necessary against the prevailing Popish Party.

It was something of this kind that got air [became widely known], and out of tenderness to Mr. Locke that my grandfather in the year 1674 sent him abroad to travel, an improvement which my grandfather was glad to add to those he had already given him.[14]

While in France, at Montpellier, the famous health resort, Locke met Thomas Herbert, Earl of Pembroke, to whom *An Essay concerning Human Understanding* was dedicated. Sir John Banks engaged Locke's services as a tutor for his son while traveling through France. In Paris Locke became acquainted with the scientist Nicholas Thoynard and with Dr. Peter Guenellon, physician of Amsterdam. It was during his journey through France that he wrote his essay *Of Study,* entering it in his *Journal* March 6, 1677.

VI *Return to England*

On his return in 1679 to London and Lord Shaftesbury (now released from the Tower of London and serving as Lord President of the Council) Locke concerned himself with the education of Lord Shaftesbury's grandson. On October 15, 1679, King Charles dismissed Shaftesbury, who was never again to return to office because of his demand for the exclusion of the Duke of York, the king's Roman Catholic brother, as successor to the throne.

After four and a half years' absence, Locke returned to Oxford at Christmas time and resumed the use of his rooms at Christ Church. Before leaving there on February 3, 1680, Locke purchased copies of Sir Robert Filmer's newly published *Patriarcha, or the Natural Power of Kings Asserted,* a classical statement of seventeenth-century Toryism which Locke's principal political work, *Two Treatises of Government* (published in 1690), rebuts. Locke's book summarized democratic principles in opposition to Filmer's defense of the divine right of kings. Shaftesbury's revolutionary movement for a Protestant succession was based in part upon those principles of political liberty.

Locke returned to London (staying at Thanet House) as Shaftesbury's physician and political advisor. In November, 1682, after his second arrest and confinement in the Tower of London and release, Shaftesbury became a political refugee in Holland; in January of the following year he died in Amsterdam.

By mid-June, 1681, Locke left for Oxford, visiting his good friend James Tyrell at Oakley in Buckinghamshire en route. While in residence at Oxford for a year and a half, he was busily engaged in literary tasks, with occasional visits to London. Because of his close connection with the late Earl of Shaftesbury, he was constantly under surveillance at Oxford; he was finally expelled from the university and forced to flee the country and seek exile in Holland (1683 - 1689). England branded him a traitor and demanded his extradition from Holland. On May 7, 1685, his friend Edward Clarke was taken into custody for his "correspondence with traitors," as many of Locke's letters from Holland were written to Clarke at great length on the upbringing of Clarke's son; these letters later formed the basis of Locke's *Some Thoughts concerning Education*, published in 1693.

VII Residence in Holland

While in Holland, Locke made the acquaintance of Anthony Van Leeuwenhoek, the scientist who first observed organisms under the microscope. He also became interested in statistics, collecting data on weather and on deaths in Amsterdam. However, in general, during his years of exile he concentrated on philosophy rather than on medicine. His association with the Genevese, Jean Le Clerc, editor of *Bibliothèque Universelle et Historique*, led to the publication of Locke's *Method of Indexing a Commonplace Book* in the second issue of the periodical, Le Clerc being the first editor to publish Locke's signed prose. *An Essay concerning Human Understanding* appeared in abstract form in Le Clerc's *Bibliothèque Universelle* in 1687 - 1688. Throughout life Locke was extremely secretive and often published works anonymously.

In 1686 Locke met William Penn, who gave him a copy of his first *Frame of Government for Pennsylvania*, dated 1682. While in Holland, Locke visited Rotterdam, Amsterdam, Leyden, and Utrecht, a center of revolutionary conspiracy for English refugees, as

Amsterdam itself was. At the end of November, 1686, Locke was ordered to leave Utrecht as an "undesirable alien." On the last day of the year of 1686, the fourth and last book of his *An Essay concerning Human Understanding,* his great philosophical masterpiece, was completed and the manuscript was posted to Clarke. By February 15, 1689, Locke's belongings were consigned to a ship for London. He had come to regard Holland as another homeland. February 20, 1689, Locke sailed for England, never to see Holland again, aboard the same ship which had in November, 1688, transported to England William of Orange and his princess Mary, who had jointly accepted the English throne. Offered an important diplomatic post at Cleves by the King, Locke firmly declined, but he accepted the modest one of Commissioner of Appeals.

VIII   *Final Years in England*

In the latter months of 1689, Locke had three books in press: *An Essay concerning Human Understanding, Two Treatises of Civil Government,* and *A Letter concerning Toleration,* though the latter two were postdated 1690 by the booksellers in order to look new longer. His major work on pedagogy, *Some Thoughts concerning Education,* is dated March 7, 1690, but was published in 1693.

In 1691 Locke took up residence with Sir Francis and Lady Masham at Oates (Essex), where he stayed intermittently until his death in 1704. He met Isaac Newton, the celebrated physicist, Whig, and Cantabridgian, who actively resisted James II's encroachments on the privileges of his university (which he represented in Parliament). Newton, who regarded science as God's workmanship, felt that as he discovered new laws he was thinking God's thoughts after him. The more he learned about the universe, the more his faith increased.

December, 1691, saw the publication of Locke's book on economics, *Some Considerations of the Consequences of the Lowering of Interest and the Raising of the Value of Money,* which, besides dealing with interest rates and the market price of money, dealt with clipped currency. English coins were traditionally made of gold or silver. Consequently it was a relatively simple matter for people to devalue the coins by clipping thin strips of metal from the edge. The versatile Locke also prepared a special edition of *Aesop's Fables,* which was designed to help children learn Latin.

The year 1692 found Locke well established as an author (and educator), already being quoted by others. In the same year, the Act for the Regulation of Printing, passed in 1662 under Charles II and enabling the state to control the press, came up for renewal by Parliament; Locke protested its renewal, not because of his opposition to censorship, as one might expect, but because he opposed the monopoly given the stationers. It was, nevertheless, renewed for two years.

Queen Mary II died in London on December 28, 1694, of smallpox, wrongly diagnosed as measles. During the first months of William's reign, Parliament again discussed the Act for the Regulation of Printing. Locke sent his arguments against renewal to Clarke before the debates about the issue of a free press began, saying:

I know not why a man should not have liberty to print whatever he would speak; and to be answerable for the one just as he is for the other, if he transgresses the law in either. But gagging a man for fear he should talk heresy or sedition, has no other ground than such as will makes gyves necessary for fear a man should use violence if his hands were free, and must at last end in the imprisonment of all who you will suspect may be guilty of treason or misdemeanor.[15]

Locke was successful, and the act was repealed. Thus freedom of the press was born in England.

The Reasonableness of Christianity (1695), anonymously written by Locke, and the subsequent attack upon it by John Edwards, a Cambridge Calvinist extremist, led to Locke's publication of *A Vindication of the Reasonableness of Christianity, etc., from Mr. Edwards's Reflections*, which also appeared in 1695. Locke belonged to the "College" club, a political sounding board through which he influenced Parliament by means of Clarke and others. He hoped to reform England's currency and persuade the Council to undertake recoinage at full value. To this end he wrote *Further Considerations concerning the Raising of the Value of Money*. Once again, the government took Locke's advice.

On May 15, 1696, Locke was appointed as a salaried commissioner on the Council of Trade and Plantations, a position he held through 1700. Although the salary was substantial, the duties were burdensome because of Locke's failing health. He became involved in a religious controversy with his former friend Edward Stillingfleet, Bishop of Worcester, who published *A Discourse in Vindication of the Trinity* (1696) in which he labeled Locke a Socinian on the basis of his *An Essay concerning Human Understanding*. (Socinianism was a rationalistic, anti-Trinitarian movement with roots in sixteenth-century Italy, originating with the Italian theologian Fausto Sozzini, his latinized name being Socinus.) As previously, Locke was vindicated, and the bishop was defeated.

When Locke retired from the Council of Trade (for reasons of health), his intention was to spend the remainder of his life in rest, study, and religious meditation. Further handicapped by deafness, he began studying the Epistles of St. Paul. His method was to copy the texts in one column and to paraphrase and make commentaries in a second column for his personal use. However, Lady Masham persuaded him to prepare these paraphrased Epistles and his comments for publication, which he did, and they appeared posthumously (1705 - 1707). Also busy consigning copies of his works to Oxford's Bodleian Library, Locke, by adding a codicil to his will (dated September 15, 1704), bequeathed copies of "all the books whereof I am the author which have been published without my name." Included were the following books:

Epistola de Tolerantia (Letter on Toleration)
A Second Letter concerning Toleration
A Third Letter for Toleration
Two Treatises of Government
The Reasonableness of Christianity
A Vindication of the Reasonableness of Christianity
A Second Vindication of the Reasonableness of Christianity

Locke, who had never married, remained in the care of the Masham family at Oates, where he continued to work and take an active interest in the world around him until his death on October 28, 1704. His epitaph, composed by Locke himself and carved on a marble tablet above his grave in the churchyard of High Laver, reads:

Near this place lies John Locke. If you wonder what kind of man he was, the answer is that he was one contented with his modest lot. A scholar by training, he devoted his studies wholly to the pursuit of truth. Such you may learn from his writings, which will also tell you whatever else there is to be said about him more faithfully than the dubious eulogies of an epitaph. His virtues, if he had any, were too slight to serve either to his own credit or as an example to you. Let his vices be interred with him. An example of virtue, you have already in the Gospels; an example of vice is something one could wish did not exist; an example of mortality (and may you learn from it) you have assuredly here and everywhere. That he was born on August 29, 1632, and died on October 28, 1704, this tablet, which itself will quickly perish, is a record.

CHAPTER 2

Locke's Philosophical Orientation

A LTHOUGH Locke's influence was great, he himself was influenced by several important thinkers, primarily Aristotle, Hobbes, and Descartes. Hegel noted that no man's thinking takes place in a vacuum but is a response arising out of theses clashing with their antitheses, resulting in new findings or syntheses. To the Hegelian dialectic, Locke was no exception. Aristotle and Descartes provided him with the stimulus necessary to fire his own thoughts.

Nor did Locke's philosophy of education (if his system of education may indeed be termed a philosophy of education, written as it was in a prephilosophical era of educational thought) arise in a vacuous intellectual atmosphere. Rather it was grounded in his fairly systematized philosophy. Accordingly his philosophical views should be examined as a prerequisite to the appreciation of his ideas on education. In educational theory, Locke's intellectual antecedents were the French thinkers François Rabelais (1494 - 1553), the humorist and satirist theologian and physician, and Michel Eyquem de Montaigne (1533 - 1592), an essayist and courtier whose literary inspiration arose from the Latin classics, particularly Plutarch.

I Law of Nature

Rousseau, who was immensely indebted to Locke for his philosophical ideas on education, predicated his entire pedagogical philosophy on educating people according to nature, a view derived from Locke. Not that the notion of living according to nature was original with Locke, for the stoics espoused that view centuries before the British philosopher, but Locke was probably the first to apply it in any deliberate and systematic manner to education. Many stoical ideas infiltrated the mind and philosophy of Locke, especially his philosophy of education. Locke's knowledge of stoicism derives from the Roman stoics, particulary Cicero, a philosopher he quotes in his *Some Thoughts concerning Education*.[1]

Hobbes and Locke. Locke was also familiar with the philosophy of a countryman of his who had much to say regarding nature, Thomas Hobbes. However, Hobbes, unlike Locke and Rousseau, held that human nature was corrupt, whereas the latter two had an elevated view of nature, including human nature. Nature, according to Hobbes, was a deplorable state that must be eradicated, whereas for Locke, the deist, it was the voice of God. Therefore the laws of nature are to be sought out and adhered to because law is nature for Locke, but for Hobbes law followed nature. For the former, morality is grounded in natural law, whereas for the latter, morality is coincident with civil law, that is, in the state of nature there is no law; hence morality emerges only with the appearance of the laws governing people. Hobbes contended that

to this war of every man against every man, this also is consequent; that nothing can be unjust. The notions of right and wrong, justice and injustice have there no place. Where there is no common power, there is no law: where no law, no injustice.[2]

In the state of nature, according to Hobbes, there is no morality, for might makes right and people are governed by the need for self-preservation. The fear arising therefrom prompts them to engage in a social contract with each other so that they become bound by laws they enact. Hence for Hobbes morality is equivalent to law, the state of nature being an amoral state of existence, or more accurately, a premoral state.

Nevertheless, Hobbes exerted considerable influence on Locke despite Locke's contention that he was not "well read" in Hobbes. The thesis of Locke's *The Reasonableness of Christianity* appears to have been extracted from Hobbes's *Leviathan;* yet Locke denies borrowing it. Locke's vehement denials may have been prompted, not from any charge of plagiarism, but from a desire to disassociate himself from philosophers such as Hobbes and Spinoza, who were held as dangerous heretics; he felt that to associate his work with that of Hobbes would result in the populace's disparagement of his own philosophy. Other resemblances between the thoughts of Locke and Hobbes that would suggest more than the accident of a mere coincidence pertain to their shared beliefs regarding hedonism or utilitarianism (the pursuit of pleasure and the avoidance of pain) and their treatment of the question of freedom. It seems reasonable to conclude, as has been done by some scholars of Locke, that not only was he acquainted with the writings of Hobbes but, while repudiating the elements of Hobbesian philosophy that did not appeal to him, he assimilated those features that reason compelled him to adopt.

Filmer and Locke. Another Englishman who had some influence on Locke was Sir Robert Filmer (d. 1653), the political writer already mentioned as the author of *Patriarcha, or the Natural Power of Kings Asserted* (1680). Locke wrote a detailed critique of Filmer, who had become a rallying-point for the Tory party during the latter part of the seventeenth century. Because of Hobbes's negative ecclesiastical views, his philosophy could not so serve the Tories, even though he defended the doctrine of the divine right of kings as the foundation of law and order. Filmer rejected the contention of Hobbes that the state arises when citizens who have been living in an anarchal state of nature — a condition of individual freedom and independence — voluntarily bind themselves together by means of a social contract. Rejecting, too, the doctrine of the equality of men (since that would justify revolution), he argued for the validity of absolute monarchy.

Anyone with a knowledge of Locke would readily realize that Filmer's influence on Locke had to be negative and antagonistic. Instead of deriving his theses from nature and experience, Filmer looked to the Bible for his patriarchal political and regressive ethical theories. He used as his paradigm Adam's monarchical power over his children, that is, the absolute right of parental or regal power over all subjects, hence political absolutism. Hobbes's original state of nature was anarchic and therefore anathema to Filmer, who espoused the theological basis for the divine right of kings instead of accepting Hobbes's man-made social contract as the justification for monarchy. Locke rejected both Hobbes's and Filmer's defenses of royal authority.

Natural Law. The expression "law of nature" did not originate with Locke, for the term was employed in the seventeenth century by two English divines and philosophers in their attack on the egoism of Hobbes: Nathanael Culverwel (d. 1651) in his *An Elegant and Learned Discourse of the Light of Nature* (1652); and Richard Cumberland (1631 - 1718) in his *A Philosophical Enquiry into the Laws of Nature: Wherein the Essence, the Principal Heads, the Order, the Publication, and the Obligation of These Laws Are Deduced from the Nature of Things; Wherein Also the Principles of Mr. Hobbes's Philosophy, Both in a State of Nature and of Civil*

Society, are Examined into and Confuted (1672). Culverwel concluded:

first, that all the moral law is founded in natural, and common light of reason; secondly, that there's nothing in the mysteries of the Gospel contrary to the light of reason, nothing repugnant to this light, that shines from "the candle of the Lord."[3]

Cumberland, like his countryman Culverwel, was a Cambridge Platonist who supplanted Hobbes's theory of egoism with his antithetical principle of universal benevolence. He argued that the greatest good of rational beings is the ground of all ethics, and for this reason some scholars claim him to be the founder of British utilitarianism. Reasoning "that different men, according to their different abilities of mind and body, nay, that the same men, in different circumstances, are not equally able to promote the public good, nevertheless, the law of nature is sufficiently observed, and its end obtained, if every one does what he is able according to his present circumstances," Cumberland concluded that

the greatest benevolence of every rational agent towards all, constitutes the happiest state of all in general and of each in particular, as far as is in their power to procure it; and is necessarily requisite in order to attain the happiest state, to which they can aspire; and therefore the common good of all is the supreme law.[4]

To these two names should be added that of Samuel Parker (1640 - 1688), an English philosopher and Bishop of Oxford, who popularized the views of Culverwel and Cumberland in his *Demonstration of the Law of Nature and of the Christian Religion* (1681). Although Locke's position on the law of nature and his utilitarianism cannot be directly traced to these sources, the probability is that he was aware of at least some of them, for it was his close friend Tyrrell who was responsible for publishing an abridged edition of Cumberland's book in 1692.

The law of nature must have reached Locke through his favorite preacher, Benjamin Whichcote (1609 - 1683), a philosophical theologian who is thought of as the probable founder of the Cambridge Platonists. The select sermons of Whichcote, published in London in 1689 with a preface by the third Earl of Shaftesbury, were recommended by Locke as masterpieces. Not only did Whichcote's

Discourses contain numerous references to the law of nature, but he also stressed religion as reason in his aphorisms and his sermons, as the sermon on "The Work of Reason" clearly enunciates: "Where a man hath not weighed and considered, searched and examined, he is nobody. If he be rational, then he discerns the reason of the thing; and the reason of the thing, if he comply with it, is religion."[5] The law of nature was identified with the law of reason, which, nevertheless, also reveals natural laws to man. Accordingly the entire tradition of the law of nature, which was so strong in intellectual circles during the time of Locke, must surely have been quite familiar to him.

II *Locke and Deism*

Such emphasis as Locke placed on the law of nature and the law of reason leads readily to the philosophy of religion known as *deism*. A rationalistic movement during the seventeenth and eighteenth centuries, deism held the view that once God had created the universe he withdrew from it, allowing it to be governed by rationally determined natural law. This view of a transcendent God who remains absent or beyond his universe is grounded on nature, reason, and morality. Nature reveals God through human reason. By ascertaining the laws of nature through the human intellect, mankind can discern the will of God and fend for himself. The deist rejects belief in miraculous or in supernatural intervention because it implies the disruption of natural laws.

Inspired by the deistic movement and occasionally identified as a deist, Locke, who was negative toward traditional Christianity and an early adherent of the deistic movement, nevertheless did endorse a number of Christian doctrines. Perhaps it would be more accurate to regard him as a forerunner of deism. Not that Locke founded deism, for it can be traced to the philosophy of another Englishman of his century, Lord Edward Herbert of Cherbury (1583 - 1648), author of *De Veritate* (1624) and *The Ancient Religion of the Gentiles* (1663). Lord Herbert, dubbed "the father of deism," sought a natural religion based on reason and free from authority. The Oxford-educated Herbert espoused views sympathetic to the Cambridge Platonists and promoted a religion apprehended by instinct. Influenced by Herbert and the Cambridge Platonists, Locke wrote:

When I had writ this, being informed that my Lord Herbert had in his book *De Veritate* assigned these innate principles, I presently consulted him, hoping to find, in a man of so great parts, something that might satisfy me in this point and put an end to my inquiry.[6]

Yet Locke's conciliatory work, *The Reasonableness of Christianity* (1695), sought a synthesis or reconciliation of traditional Christianity with the deistic view. In the opening paragraph of that work, he delineated the two antithetical views:

While some men would have all Adam's posterity doomed to eternal, infinite punishment, for the transgression of Adam, who millions had never heard of, and no one had authorised to transact for him, or be his representative; this seemed to others so little consistent with the justice or goodness of the great and infinite God, that they thought there was no redemption necessary, and consequently, there was none; rather than admit of it upon a supposition so derogatory to the honour and attributes of that infinite Being; and so made Jesus Christ nothing but the restorer and preacher of pure natural religion.[7]

Also prevalent among the deists was a hedonistic or utilitarian theory of ethics.

III *Epistemological Views*

The richest source of Locke's theory of knowledge is found in his *Essay concerning Human Understanding;* despite its title, the human understanding is only incidentally given any treatment, the first two books dealing with ideas, the third with words, and the last with the theory of knowledge and probability. The book's misnomer is probably attributable to the enormous importance accorded the understanding in Locke's time and his anxiousness to grapple with the subject. He addressed himself to the subject in more than one book, as his *Of the Conduct of the Understanding* testifies. This latter book, or tract, was initially intended as a supplemental chapter to the *Essay.*

The Coherence Criterion of Truth. Knowledge, for Locke, was the agreement or disagreement of ideas as contained in the understanding, or as they cohere in the light of reason. Knowledge occurs in two stages: (1) the acquisition of ideas and (2) reason's grasp of the relations among the ideas. Ideas lack certainty without reason or understanding, but on the other hand, both reason and understanding are devoid of certainty without ideas. Not ideas per se, but their relationships or cohering as grasped by reason is genuine knowledge. Knowledge is absent in the mere presence of these relationships of ideas until they are observed by reason. The two elements of ideas together with their relationships and the reason's cognizance of them constitute the essence of true knowledge. "Knowledge then seems to me to be nothing but the perception of the connexion and agreement, or disagreement and repugnancy, of any of our ideas," and truth Locke defined as *"the joining or separating of signs, as the things signified by them do agree or disagree one with another."*[8]

Truth and falsity properly relate to propositions. The appearance of ideas in the mind cannot be said to be true or false, unless they are said to refer to something, such as the ideas of other men, real existence, or supposed real essences. Simple ideas may be considered false in reference to others. Thus an idea per se is not true or false; it is only false when it is (1) judged agreeable with another person's idea when it actually is not, (2) judged in agreement with reality when it actually is not, (3) judged adequate when it actually is not, or (4) judged as representing real essence when it fails to do so. It would be more accurate to refer to ideas as being right or wrong rather than true or false.

The Genesis of Ideas. Without pausing to consider and define ideas, Locke proceeded to trace them to their source. Prompted by the Cartesian philosophy of innate ideas, Locke was eager to address the problem by exposing the inadequacies of the French nativist. Once finding himself immersed in the issue, he neglected to return to an analysis and definition of ideas. His apology, offered in "The Epistle to the Reader" prefaced to the book, reads as follows:

Some hasty and undigested thoughts, on a subject I had never before considered, which I set down against our next meeting, gave the first entrance into this discourse, which having been thus begun by chance, was continued by entreaty; written by incoherent parcels; and, after long intervals of neglect, resumed again, as my humour or occasions permitted; and at last, in a retirement, where an attendance on my health gave me leisure, it was brought into that order thou now seest it.[9]

The entire first book, dealing with the subject of Cartesian innate ideas, argues against their existence. Locke felt that for people to be receptive toward his empiricism, it was necessary to eliminate the stronghold of innate ideas. His first book informs the reader how ideas do *not originate;* his second book investigates the problem of how they *do arise.* He postulated two sources of ideas: sensation and reflection.

First, our senses, conversant about particular sensible objects, do convey into the mind several distinct perceptions of things, according to those various ways wherein those objects do affect them; and thus we come by those *ideas* we have of *yellow, white, heat, cold, soft, hard, bitter, sweet,* and all those which we call sensible qualities; which when I say the senses convey into the mind, I mean, they from external objects convey into the mind what produces there those *perceptions.* This great source of most of the *ideas* we have, depending wholly upon our senses, and derived by them to the understanding, I call, SENSATION.

Secondly, the other fountain from which experience furnisheth the understanding with *ideas* is the *perception of the operations of our own mind; within us,* as it is employed about the *ideas* it has got. . . . And such are *perception, thinking, doubting, believing, reasoning, knowing, willing,* and all the different actings of our own mind; which we, being conscious of, and observing in ourselves, do from these receive into our understandings as distinct ideas, as we do from bodies affecting our senses. . . . But as I call the other *sensation,* so I call this REFLECTION, the ideas it affords being such only as the mind gets by reflecting on its own operations within itself. . . . These two, I say, viz., external material things as the objects of SENSATION, and the operations of our own minds within as the objects of REFLECTION, are, to me, the only originals from whence all our ideas take their beginnings.[10]

Reflection is an internal sense, deriving ideas from a source within the individual.

In time, the mind comes to reflect on its own *operations* about the *ideas* got by *sensation* and thereby stores itself with a new set of *ideas,* which I call *ideas* of *reflection.* These are the *impressions* that are made on our *senses* by outward objects that are extrinsical to the mind; and *its own operations,* proceeding from powers intrinsical and proper to itself, which when reflected on by itself become also objects of its contemplation. These two are as I have said, *the original of all knowledge.* Thus the first capacity of human intellect is that the mind is fitted to receive the impressions made on it either through the *senses* by outward objects, or by its own operations when it *reflects* on them.[11]

In receiving ideas, the mind is passive. Simple ideas which the mind can neither create nor destroy, are uncompounded appearances. Thus, not all ideas are alike; some are simple, others complex. "When the understanding is once stored with these simple *ideas,* it has the power to repeat, compare, and unite them, even to an almost infinite variety, and so can make at pleasure new complex *ideas.*"[12]

Primary and Secondary Qualities. Locke also spoke of qualities, that is, the power responsible for the idea's emergence.

Whatsoever the mind perceives in itself, or is the immediate object of perception, thought, or understanding, that I call *idea;* and the power to produce any *idea* in our mind, I call *quality* of the subject wherein that power is. Thus a snowball having the power to produce in us the *ideas* of *white, cold,* and *round,* the power to produce those *ideas* in us as they are in the snowball I call *qualities.*[13]

Qualities, in turn, are dual: some are primary, others secondary. Whereas the primary include solidity, extension, figure, and motion, the secondary, which are psychological in character, include color, sound, taste, smell, touch, etc. To these Locke hesitantly added what he thought might be a third, namely, *power.* Power, a causal quality or kind of force, is exemplified by the consequences of fire. "For, the power in fire to produce a new colour or consistency in wax or clay, by its primary qualities, is as much a quality in fire, as the power it has to produce in me a new *idea* or sensation of warmth or burning, which I felt not before, by the same primary qualities, viz., the bulk, texture, and motion of its insensible parts."[14] Thus power is that by which changes are produced.

The mind possesses the power of *abstraction* whereby it "makes the particular *ideas* received from particular objects to become general."[15] The mind creates complex ideas from the simple ones, resulting in modes, substances, and relations. A *simple mode* results from a variation or combination of the same simple idea, as in combining a single object into a dozen of the same object. The idea of *substances* results from combining simple ideas about specific objects subsisting by themselves; thus simple ideas of weight, hardness, ductility, and fusibility are combined into the idea of lead as a substance. A *relation* results from pairing one idea with another, as in comparing a horizontal line in a geometrical figure with a perpendicular one.

Metaphysical Agnosticism. Locke, a metaphysical agnostic because he held that one is unable to know ultimate reality, argued that substance must be assumed. "Not imagining how these simple *ideas* can subsist by themselves, we accustom ourselves to suppose some *substratum* wherein they do subsist, and from which they do result; which therefore we call *substance.*"[16] Viewing substance as I-know-not-what, Locke pleaded agnosticism rather than skepticism.

Inasmuch as substance is considered to be some basic reality other than the sense qualities characterizing the object as well as being other than its extension, figure, solidity, and motion, then it must remain a *je-ne-sais-quoi* and be regarded merely as that which lends support to primary and secondary qualities. He depicted belief in substance as comparable to the reasoning of an Indian who

saying that the world was supported by a great elephant, was asked, what the elephant rested on? to which his answer was, "A great tortoise;" but being again pressed to know what gave support to the broad-backed tortoise, replied, *something, he knew not what* . . . we talk like children; who, being questioned what such a thing is which they know not, readily give this satisfactory answer, — that it is *something;* which in truth signifies no more, when so used, either by children or men, but that they know not what; and that the thing they pretend to know and talk of, is what they have no distinct *idea* of at all, and so are perfectly ignorant of it, and in the dark. The *idea*, then, we have, to which we give the general name *substance*, being nothing but the supposed, but unknown, support of those qualities we find existing, which we imagine cannot subsist *sine re substante*, "without something to support them," we call that support *substantia;* which, according to the true import of the word, is, in plain English, *standing under*, or *upholding*.[17]

Locke was forced to conclude that substance is merely "a collection of a certain number of simple ideas, considered as united in one thing."[18] Consequently the idea of substance is "a supposed I-know-not-what . . . to support those *ideas* we call accidents."[19]

Association Psychology. A major contribution to the psychology of learning, which is still quite prevalent in contemporary theories of learning among psychologists, is Locke's *"association of ideas."* Noting that ideas have a natural correspondence and connection with one another, Locke observed that there is also a

connexion of *ideas* wholly owing to chance or custom. *ideas*, that in themselves are not at all of kin, come to be so united in some men's minds that it is very hard to separate them; they always keep in company, and the one no sooner at any time comes into the understanding but its associate appears with it; and if they are more than two which are thus united, the whole gang, always inseparable, show themselves together.[20]

Association theory was not novel with Locke, originating probably with Aristotle and finding its way to Hobbes before it reached Locke. Linking association to the cohering of former ideas, Hobbes stated that the *cause* of the *coherence* or consequence of one conception to another, is their first coherence or consequence at that time when they are produced by sense: as for example, from St. Andrew the mind runneth to St. Peter, because their names are read together; from St. Peter to a *stone*, for the same cause; from *stone* to *foundation*, because we see them together; and for the same cause, from foundation to church, and from church to people, and from people to tumult: and according to this example, the mind may run almost from anything to anything.[21]

Associationism exerted a potent influence in British psychology, especially during the eighteenth century, and currently holds an important place in neobehavioristic form in contemporary psychology. Associationism is defined simply as the theory that the mind is composed of simple elements (ideas) that derive from experience, and that the ideas cohere because one idea is associated with another.

Nominalism. Locke's theory of ideas is a type of nominalism (since the general or abstract idea is a mere name or composition of simple ideas) that terminates in subjectivism inasmuch as knowledge is never knowledge of reality (for substance is an I-know-not-what) but only knowledge of the relations of ideas. Since knowledge extends no further than one's ideas, it follows that what fails to fall within the domain of an idea is not a candidate for thought.

Locke's metaphysical agnosticism prevented him from taking the step into idealism, the view that primary and secondary qualities are mental in character and that therefore reality is ideal. This logical step was taken by his intellectual successor in the British empirical movement, the Irish philosopher George Berkeley, who asserted that for a thing to be real it must be perceived, that *esse* is *percipi*. Hence only spirits (minds) and their perceptions exist. The Scottish philosopher David Hume, following in this same tradition of British empiricism, disagreed with Bishop Berkeley's idealism and retreated to metaphysical skepticism, but not to the agnosticism or skepticism of Locke. Hume advocated phenomenalism, the belief that only perceptions exist because there is no ultimate reality. In sum, Locke claimed that ultimate reality cannot be brought within the scope of human knowledge, whereas Hume contended it cannot be known because it does not exist; only the phenomenal objects of human experience exist for Hume. Unlike Berkeley, Hume repudiated the belief in a soul as a reality and viewed it merely as a "bundle of perceptions." Hume argued:

For my part, when I enter most intimately into what I call *myself*, I always stumble on some particular perception or other, of heat or cold, light or

shade, love or hatred, pain or pleasure. I never can catch myself at any time without a perception, and never can observe any thing but the perception. . . .
I may venture to affirm of the rest of mankind, that they are nothing but a bundle or collection of different perceptions.[22]

The ideas of these three philosophers found their way into contemporary philosophy, Locke's into empiricism, Berkeley's into idealism and personalism, and Hume's into logical positivism. Hume's phenomenalism was prompted by the Lockean theory that human knowledge is limited to the observation of the agreement and disagreement of ideas with one another, and does not encompass metaphysical (ultimate) reality or even classes of objects except ideas. Like Kant, who followed, Locke held to an ultimate reality, but also like Kant he assumed an agnostic stance toward it, claiming that it is unknowable (I-know-not-what). Kant, because he also viewed this ultimate thing-in-itself as unknowable, terminated his epistemology in an agnosticism termed Kantian positivism.
Although Locke was a metaphysical agnostic, unlike Hume he was not a nihilist, since he did believe in the existence of ultimate reality — for example, in the existence of God. Edward Stillingfleet,[23] sensing this inconsistency in Locke's philosophy, which resulted from Locke's ambiguous use of the term "ideas," maintained that God's existence is a fact above and beyond the entire realm of human ideas. He therefore concluded that reason transcends ideas, that it can directly ascertain extra ideational objective reality. Locke did not attempt to refute Stillingfleet's objection, which he regarded merely as criticism of his terminology; he offered as his only defense his original premise that anyone who thinks does so with ideas. Unlike Berkeley, Locke, however, did believe in nonmental realities, the existence of nonideational objects. Ideas, therefore, assume an intermediary position between ultimate objects and the mind; the mind utilizes ideas to depict the ultimate or metaphysical reality. He commented as follows in dialogue:

Knowledge, say you, is only the perception of the agreement or disagreement of our own *ideas;* but who knows what those *ideas* may be? Is there any thing so extravagant as the imaginations of men's brains? . . . It is no matter how things are: so a man observe but the agreement of his own imaginations, and talk conformably, it is all truth, all certainty. Such castles in the air will be as strongholds of truth as the demonstrations of *Euclid.* . . .
It is evident the mind knows not things immediately, but only by the intervention of the *ideas* it has of them. *Our knowledge,* therefore, is *real* only so far as there is a *conformity* between our *ideas* and the reality of things.[24]

Now Locke raises two critical questions: "But what shall be here the criterion?" and "How shall the mind, when it perceives nothing but its own *ideas*, know that they agree with things themselves?"[25] It was this point that Berkeley seized upon to establish his idealism by contending that the mind can know only that which is of the nature of mind; hence for a thing to be it must be of the same character or stuff of experience.

Representative   Realism   or   Representationalism. Locke's philosophy impelled him to accept representationalism or representative realism, an epistemological dualistic theory, which holds that the objects of reality are not directly presented to the human mind but are mediated through ideas, that is, they are first reduced to ideas, and it is only these ideas (not ultimate reality itself) that are known. Thus reality is reduced to mental or ideational form before reaching the individual's mind. Reality is therefore *re*-presented into the mind in a form (idea) differing from the original (the ultimately real object, i.e., substance). Locke noted that ideas of substance have a double reference:

(1) Sometimes they are referred to a supposed real essence of each species of things. (2) Sometimes they are only designed to be pictures and representations in his mind of things that do exist, by *ideas* of those qualities that are discoverable in them. In both which ways these copies of those originals and achetypes *are* imperfect and *inadequate.*[26]

Locke was criticized for shifting back and forth from one definition of knowledge to another: first defining knowledge as mere agreement between ideas, and then defining it as agreement between ideas and things themselves. He no longer adhered to his original view that only ideas can be known, which implies that real things cannot be known, for he wished to maintain a position of metaphysical realism, the belief in the ontological reality of the objects of ideas rather than admitting that knowledge is imaginary, unreal, or chimerical. He hesitated to take the next logical step, taken by Berkeley, into idealism. Instead, he held resolutely to his conception of nonideational substance as ontologically real.

IV   *Ethical Theory*

Inasmuch as Locke placed great emphasis upon virtue in his educational theory, it is advisable to examine his moral philosophy. Owing to his epistemological orientation, he was committed to rationalism in ethical theory, concluding that ethical knowledge is rationally derived. Thus Locke's empiricism is amalgamated with rationalism, but not that of the continental rationalists antedating him, since for Locke the faculty of reason is not a composite of infallible principles; rather, he regards reason as the capacity to recognize the agreement or disagreement of ideas. Ethics therefore is a set of principles arrived at by providing reason with empirical data with which to operate.

Although moral ideas are "the creatures of the understanding rather than the works of nature," they are not to be dismissed as mere fancy, for they are "real essences." As real essences, they have acquired universal terminology, that is, class terms, but they are all derived from sense experience and reflection. Like any other propositions, moral rules are grounded in the perception of agreement or disagreement among ideas. *"Moral truth"* Locke defined as "speaking things according to the persuasion of our own minds, though the proposition we speak agree not to the reality of things."[27] Because ethics, like mathematics, treats principles rather than facts, it can be demonstratively proved. "Upon this ground it is that I am bold to think that *morality is capable of demonstration,* as well as mathematics; since the precise real essence of the things moral words stand for may be perfectly known, and so the congruity or incongruity of the things themselves be certainly discovered, in which consists perfect knowledge."[28] By ascertaining connections among complex ideas, a system of morality is constructed. However, "*moral ideas* are commonly more complex than those of the figures ordinarily considered in mathematics."[29] Berkeley, who felt that Locke had unduly minimized the importance of ethical terms, disparagingly remarked: "To demonstrate morality it seems one need only make a dictionary of words, and see which included which. At least, this is the greatest part and bulk of the work. Locke's instances of demonstration in morality are, according to his own rule, trifling propositions."[30]

Morality deals with abstract ideas (Locke's "mixed modes"), such as the ideas of murder, adultery, justice, gratitude, glory, ambition. *"Mixed modes are made by the understanding. . . .* These *essences of the species of mixed modes* are not only *made* by the mind, but made *very arbitrarily,* made without patterns, or reference to any real existence."[31]

Hedonism and Utilitarianism. Locke's hedonism appears to stem from three sources: (1) the eudaimonism of Aristotle, (2) the hedonism of Hobbes, and (3) deism. In his stress on happiness, maintaining that all seek it and identifying it as the greatest good, Locke follows in the tracks of Aristotle. When Locke defined good and evil as corresponding to, and commensurate with, pleasure and pain, he was emulating Hobbesian ethical theory. With the deists, Locke tied virtue to obeying God's will, conformity to which eventuates in utilitarian rewards and happiness.

Everyone desires happiness, the greatest good; it functions as his motivation.

If it be further asked, what it is moves *desire?* I answer: happiness, and that alone. . . . *Happiness,* then, in its full extent, is the utmost pleasure we are capable of, and *misery* the utmost pain; and the lowest degree of what can be called *happiness* is so much ease from all pain, and so much present pleasure, as without which anyone cannot be content. . . . What has an aptness to produce pleasure in us is that we call *good,* and what is apt to produce pain in us we call *evil,* for no other reason but for its aptness to produce pleasure and pain in us, wherein consists our *happiness* and *misery.*[32]

Locke's hedonism consists in his defining happiness in terms of pleasure; otherwise his system would more appropriately be termed eudaemonism, comparable to Aristotle's. However, the hedonism of Locke is not the quantitative hedonism of Bentham or Aristippus and the Cyrenaics, but the ideal utilitarianism or qualitative hedonism of John Stuart Mill, because Locke contended that "there is pleasure in knowledge."[33] Hence not all pleasure is sensual, nor is pleasure limited to sensual voluptuousness.

Now let one man place his satisfaction in sensual pleasures, another in the delight of knowledge: though each of them cannot but confess there is great pleasure in what the other pursues, yet, neither of them making the other's delight a part of his happiness, their *desires* are not moved, but each is satisfied without what the other enjoys; and so his will is not determined to the pursuit of it. But yet, as soon as the studious man's hunger and thirst make him *uneasy,* he whose *will* was never determined to any pursuit of good cheer, poignant sauces, delicious wine, by the pleasant taste he has found in them is, by the *uneasiness* of hunger and thirst, presently determined to eating and drinking, though possibly with great indifference, what wholesome food comes his way. And, on the other side, the epicure buckles to study, when shame or the desire to recommend himself to his mistress shall make him *uneasy* in the want of any sort of knowledge.[34]

One aspect distinguishing Locke's hedonism from that of Hobbes is that, whereas Locke related pleasure and pain to human mental functioning, claiming they were the results of thoughts or subjective states of mind, Hobbes maintained that they were internal physical motions either of harmony or conflict. Mind, which is in Locke's view as important as body in enjoying pleasure or suffering pain, was not so regarded by Hobbes, who viewed the process as a bodily function. Locke explained:

Things then are good or evil only in reference to pleasure or pain. That we call *good* which *is apt to cause or increase pleasure, or diminish pain in us, or else to procure or preserve us the possession of any other good or absence of any evil.* And, on the contrary, we name that *evil* which *is apt to produce or increase any pain, or diminish any pleasure in us, or else to procure us any evil, or deprive us of any good.* By pleasure and pain, I must be understood to mean of body or mind, as they are commonly distinguished, though in truth they be only different constitutions of the mind, sometimes occasioned by disorder in the body, sometimes by thoughts of the mind.[35]

Note that Locke regards pleasure and pain as actually "different states of the mind," rather than physical states as Hobbes (the hedonist) and Bentham (the utilitarian) did.

Locke's utilitarian ethic is evident from entries in his *Journal,* in which a hint of psychological hedonism appears. "Happiness and misery," he wrote, "are the two great springs of human actions, and though through different ways we find men so busy in the world, they all aim at happiness, and desire to avoid misery, as it appears to them in different places and shapes."[36] An ethical hedonist, Locke held that a person is morally obligated to pursue happiness, while escaping pain: "It is a man's proper business to seek happiness and avoid pain."[37] Happiness he defined as "what delights and contents the mind; misery, is what disturbs, discomposes, or torments it."[38] The individual's ethical duty is to see to his happiness. "I will therefore make it my business to seek satisfaction and delight, and avoid uneasiness and disquiet; to have as much of the one, and as little of the other, as may be."[39] Accordingly a person must guard against the loss of lasting happiness by erroneously accepting a brief pleasure. "I must have a care I mistake not; for if I prefer a short pleasure to a lasting one, it is plain I cross my own happiness."[40] What then are the more durable pleasures? Locke replied (1) health, (2) reputation, (3) knowledge, (4) doing good, and (5) hope of eternal happiness in the life hereafter. "The expectation of eternal and incomprehensible happiness in another world is that also which carries a constant pleasure with it."[41]

Thus for Locke the *summum bonum* is happiness, and "pain, or dolor of body and mind,"[42] the *summum malum*. "To make a man virtuous, three things are necessary: 1st. Natural parts and disposition. 2nd. Precepts and instruction. 3rd. Use and practice; which is able better to correct the first, and improve the latter."[43]

The great ethical schools emanating from Aristotle were in Locke's estimation of little value because rather than teaching morality they merely identified moral terms. Moral actions, on the other hand, are contingent upon "the choice of an understanding and free agent."[44]

Psychology of Emotions. Even emotions were reduced to the state of ideas for Locke. Passions, for Locke, possess moral, or, more accurately, axiological, value. He reasoned that good and evil, the causes of pleasure and pain, are the foundations on which passions are based.

Joy is a delight of the mind. . . .
Sorrow is uneasiness in the mind upon the thought of a good lost. . . .
Hope is that pleasure in the mind which everyone finds in himself upon the thought of a profitable future enjoyment. . . .
Fear is an uneasiness of the mind upon the thought of future evil likely to befall us.
Despair is the thought of the unattainableness of any good. . . .
Anger is uneasiness or discomposure of the mind upon the receipt of any injury. . . .
Envy is an uneasiness of mind, caused by the consideration of a good we desire obtained by one we think should not have had it before us.[45]

Although all of the above are associated with pain or pleasure, anger and envy imply the involvement of others as well as oneself and hence may be characteristics absent in some persons, whereas the remainder are found in everyone. "We *love, desire, rejoice,* and *hope* only in respect of pleasure; we *hate, fear,* and *grieve* only in respect of pain ultimately; in fine, all these passions are moved by things only as they appear to be the causes of pleasure and pain."[46]

Moral Relations, Mixed Modes, and Virtue. Having identified good and evil as occasioning or procuring pleasure and pain, Locke was in a position to define morality.

Moral good and *evil*, then, is only the conformity or disagreement of our voluntary actions to some law, whereby good or evil is drawn on us from the will and power of the law-maker; which good and evil, pleasure or pain, attending our observance or breach of the law by the decree of the law-maker, is that we call *reward* and *punishment*.[47]

A moral relation is one of conformity or disagreement of a person's voluntary actions with a moral rule serving as a criterion of morality. When a person frames distinct complex ideas regarding his moral actions, these are considered *mixed modes*, many of them being accompanied by moral terms, such as obligation, lying, etc. Mixed modes are complex ideas comprising a number of combinations of simple ideas of various kinds.

Moral rules, or laws governing moral behavior, that is, criteria by which people judge the "rectitude or pravity" of their moral actions, Locke reduced to three: "(1) The *divine* law. (2) The *civil* law. (3) The law of *opinion* or *reputation*. . . . By the relation they bear to the first of these, men judge whether their actions are sins or duties; by the second, whether they be criminal or innocent; and by the third, whether they be virtues or vices."[48] Although Locke regarded these as criteria of the right act, they are more closely related to what Jeremy Bentham and John Stuart Mill termed "sanctions," that which enjoins one to perform the right act.

The first of these moral rules, the divine law, is God's law enjoining men to be guided in their actions by the "light of nature," or the "voice of revelation." The two, which are equivalent for Locke, are equated with reason.

Reason is natural *revelation*, whereby the eternal Father of light and fountain of all knowledge communicates to mankind that portion of truth which he has laid within the reach of their natural faculties; *revelation* is natural *reason* enlarged by a new set of discoveries communicated by GOD immediately, which *reason* vouches the truth of, by the testimony and proofs it gives that they come from GOD.[49]

Thus Locke grounded his ethics on reason, and reason he coupled to revelation. Law, reason, nature, and revelation are all integrally intertwined.

The second moral rule or sanction is the civil law of the commonwealth, which, if broken, results in punishment, such as the taking away of "life, liberty, or goods from him who disobeys."[50] The third, the law of opinion or reputation, is covert coercion arising from public censorship, adverse public opinion, or concern with what people may think of one.

> Thus the measure of what is everywhere called and esteemed *virtue* and *vice* is the approbation or dislike, praise or blame, which by a secret and tacit consent establishes itself in the several societies, tribes, and clubs of men in the world, whereby several actions come to find credit or disgrace amongst them according to the judgment, maxims, or fashions of that place. For though men, uniting into politic societies, have resigned up to the public the disposing of all their force, so that they cannot employ it against any fellow-citizen any further than the law of the country directs, yet they retain still the power of thinking well or ill, approving or disapproving of the actions of those whom they live amongst and converse with; and by this approbation and dislike they establish amongst themselves what they will call *virtue* and *vice*.[51]

The Scottish philosopher David Hume later constructed a sizable portion of his ethical theory on the Lockean ethical doctrine of approbation and disapprobation.

Rather than enunciating a list of moral rules or a code of ethics, Locke deferred to the ethics of Jesus, considering his injunctions superb. "The gospel contains so perfect a body of ethics, that reason may be excused from that inquiry, since she may find man's duty clearer and easier in revelation, than in herself."[52] This sentiment, respecting the ethics of Jesus as a superlative code, Locke reiterated on numerous occasions.

The utilitarian Locke saw the end of life or "the business of men" as being

> happy in this world by the enjoyment of the things of nature subservient to life, health, ease, and pleasure, and by the comfortable hopes of another life when this is ended; and in the other world by an accumulation of higher degrees of bliss in an everlasting security; we need no other knowledge for the attainment of those ends but of the history and observation of the effects and operations of natural bodies within our power, and of our duties in the management of our own actions as far as they depend upon our will.[53]

CHAPTER 3

Empiricism: An Essay concerning Human Understanding

L OCKE'S philosophy of education was based upon his conviction that only a well-planned program of life experience can mold human intelligence and character. Born possessing no intellectual inheritance of ideas, each individual must depend upon experience for all aspects of his development, mental and physical. Hence Locke's repeated references to "a sound mind in a sound body."[1]

The general aim of education should be to produce "*mens sana in corpore sano*"[12] ("a sound mind in a sound body"), wrote Locke to his friend Edward Clarke as one of the first bits of advice for the education of Clarke's eldest son. This dictum became Locke's opening statement in his principal work on the philosophy of education, *Some Thoughts concerning Education* (1693). Considering a sound mind in a sound body to be "the most desirable state we are capable of in this life,"[3] Locke concluded that the person in possession of both requires little else, whereas the person lacking either will not be fit for anything.

Education was for Locke of utmost importance since by it a person's life is shaped so that his happiness lies at his own disposal. "Men's happiness or misery is for the most part of their own making. He whose mind directs not wisely will never take the right way; and he whose body fails his mind will never be able to march in it."[4] Although a person's constitution, both physical and mental, can possibly play a role in achieving excellence, the success of his efforts is decidedly determined by what his education has made of him. Rare is the person whose achievements in life are attributable to a naturally vigorous constitution.

I confess there are some men's constitutions of body and mind so vigorous, and well framed by nature, that they shift pretty well without much assistance from others; by the strength of their natural genius, they are, from their cradles, carried towards what is excellent. But those examples are but few, and I think I may say of all the men we meet with, nine parts of ten, or perhaps ninety-nine of one hundred, are what they are, good or evil, useful or not, by their education. 'Tis that which makes the great difference in mankind.[5]

For Locke to assess the learning experience so highly, and constitutional factors so minimally, coheres perfectly with his basic philosophy of empiricism as elaborated in his *magnum opus, An Essay concerning Human Understanding* (1690). It is advisable to familiarize oneself with the tenets of that classic *Essay* in order to appreciate the philosophical orientation from which Locke argues to support his philosophy of education.

I An Essay concerning Human Understanding

Locke's famous essay on the understanding, basically a work on epistemology and metaphysics, was begun many years before its appearance in print in 1690. It was a carefully thought out effort, which underwent many revisions after being submitted to close friends for scrutiny and evaluation. As Locke's thoughts matured and crystallized, he recorded them, a procedure typical of the great philosopher, who was past fifty years of age when his important works made their appearance. Locke was over sixty when his *Some Thoughts concerning Education* was published, and was rather close to that age when the monumental *Essay concerning Human Understanding* had its first edition. His meticulous concern for careful thought and his mature judgment were reflected in the *Essay,* which, through its scores of editions and translations, raised fundamental problems of philosophy that have challenged all modern philosophers. Owing to the fact that Locke's *Essay* was written over a great number of years with frequent revisions, it suffers from repetitiousness and prolixity.

The *Essay* displays a dichotomization of experience (epistemology) and reality (metaphysics), that is, ideas grounded in experience, and reality (and knowledge) extending beyond the bounds of experience.

Epistemology: Empiricism. It was noted above that Locke was influenced by Descartes, particularly in the sense that Descartes sent him on his philosophical route in a dual manner. Not only did Descartes rescue Locke from the Aristotelian rut in which Oxford philosophy was mired, but he was the necessary stimulant that caused intellectual rebellion in Locke against Cartesian rationalism. Thus Locke's rebellion incited by Descartes was against both his own Aristotelian, or Oxford philosophy, and against Cartesianism too.

Whereas Descartes proceeded on the theory that a person enters life with knowledge (as did his ancient Greek predecessors in philosophy, Socrates and Plato), Locke took the route of Aristotle by arguing that there is nothing in the mind which was not first in the senses. Thus the primary question is, Is a person born with knowledge or without knowledge?

The Cartesian thesis, grounded on *Cogito, ergo sum* ("I think, therefore I am"), held that *innate ideas* (knowledge or a form of learning) were present in the human mind at birth. "But among these ideas," said Descartes, "some appear to me to be innate, others adventitious, and others to be made by myself (factitious); for, as I have the power of conceiving what is called a thing, or a truth, or a thought, it seems to me that I hold this power from no other source than my own nature."[6] Among these inborn notions was: *Ex nihilo nihil fit* ("Out of nothing nothing comes"), that is, the mind will not accept a contingent fact as being uncaused whether or not he was present during its inception. For example, no person was present when certain animals came into existence, yet the mind will not allow itself to think that these animals came into being without a cause. Descartes argued as follows:

When we apprehend that it is impossible a thing can arise from nothing, this proposition, *ex nihilo nihil fit*, is not considered as somewhat existing, or as the mode of a thing, but as an eternal truth having its seat in our mind, and is called a common notion or axiom. Of this class are the following: — It is impossible the same thing can at once be and not be; what is done cannot be undone, he who thinks must exist while he thinks; and innumerable others.[7]

Descartes held that the idea of God also was innate, for the reason that no one has experienced him, yet everyone has a conception of him, an argument referred to by philosophers as the ontological argument for the existence of God.

Cogito, ergo sum was classified as an innate idea because no facts are required to arrive at this conclusion; merely possessing a human mind suffices. By "I think, therefore I am" Descartes held that the proof of the soul, or mind (the two were interchangeable terms for Descartes), is certain knowledge, innately given, because it is indubitable. That is, to doubt one's own existence results in proving it. For example, if I should say to myself: "I doubt that I exist," something repugnant results, asserted Descartes. I am confronted with the question: "Who then is doing the doubting?" At least he must exist in order to doubt. Since I am the one doing the doubting, then I must exist. In other words, to doubt is to think, to think is to exist. Suppose someone should counter the Cartesian argument with: "But there is I know not what being, who is possessed at once of the highest power and the deepest cunning, who is constantly employing all his ingenuity in deceiving me."[8] It would not weaken Descartes's argument, for he gleefully retorted:

Let him deceive me as he may, he can never bring it about that I am nothing, so long as I shall be conscious that I am something. So that it must, in fine, be maintained, all things being maturely and carefully considered, that this proposition: I am, I exist, is necessarily true each time it is expressed by me, or conceived in my mind.[9]

Such is the intellectual background against which Locke was reacting when he developed his educational and epistemological theories.

The Mind as a Tabula Rasa *("Blank Tablet").* Repudiating Descartes, Locke contended that all ideas derive from sensation or reflection. Idea, an object of thinking, is exemplified by (1) sense perceptions, such as those of whiteness, sweetness, motion, and hardness and (2) mental operations, such as those of perceiving, willing, doubting, etc. All ideas originate from experience, hence the empiricism of Locke. Locke himself, however, never employed the *term* "empiricism," a word of later coinage.

The human mind, according to Locke, is a white paper or blank tablet on which the various sensations make their imprints, called ideas. Without these sensations a person's mind would be a total blank. "Let us then suppose," postulated Locke,

the mind to be, as we say, white paper void of all characters, without any *ideas.* How comes it to be furnished? Whence comes it by that vast store which the busy and boundless fancy of man has painted on it with an almost endless variety? Whence has it all the materials of reason and knowledge? To this I answer, in one word, from *experience;* in that all our knowledge is founded, and from that it ultimately derives itself. Our observation, employed either about *external sensible objects, or about the internal operations of our minds perceived and reflected on by ourselves, is that which supplies our understandings with all the materials of thinking.* These two are the fountains of knowledge, from whence all the *ideas* we have, or can naturally have, do spring.[10]

This Lockean thesis of radical empiricism found its way into his philosophy of education as early as 1684, six years prior to the publication of his famous *Essay*. In providing instruction for the education of Clarke's son, Locke noted that "the little and almost insensible impressions, on our tender infancies, have very important and lasting influences."[11] This observation by Locke anticipated what Sigmund Freud had to say about the lasting effects of very early childhood experiences. However, in Locke's statement the point of interest that reflects the influence of his empiricism upon educational theory is the claim that the minutest sensations, even those almost imperceptible, have a definite, permanent effect upon the learning process. Consequently one must be on guard to take into account such experiences which superficially may appear to have no educational consequences.

Locke's view of the mind as a passive recipient of impressions proved to be quite influential in philosophy and education. Not only did it provide some philosophers, including the great French philosopher Étienne Bonnot de Condillac (1715 - 1780), with a basis for the philosophy of sensationalism, but it also found favor among religious and secular educators as well as civic authorities owing to its profound implications. If the Lockean empirical premise were true, then, simply by exposing children to salutary influences and shielding them from unsavory ones, it would be possible to rear moral giants and perfect citizens. Education would become merely a matter of determining what experiences a child should be exposed to and eliminating all deleterious experiential influences.

For Locke's hypothesis to be valid would require complete rejection and disproof of the Cartesian hypothesis of innate ideas. For if one does indeed have knowledge at birth, the implication is that educational training and experience do not have the potent effect that Locke claimed for them. Under these circumstances the most that Locke could claim would be that experience can affect a person's constitution, his mental makeup, but at best only to a very limited extent. In order to protect his position Locke set out to repudiate the assumption that knowledge exists within the individual at birth as implied by Cartesian theory.

Attack on Innate Ideas. Virtually the entire first book of *An Essay concerning Human Understanding* is devoted to rejecting the validity of innate ideas. Locke's intent in writing this work is "to inquire into the original, certainty, and extent of human knowledge, together with the grounds and degrees of belief, opinion, and assent."[12] Thus Locke's effort is an epistemological one, an attempt to delineate the extent and scope of human knowledge. He formulated his method as follows:

> *First,* I shall inquire into the *original* of those *ideas,* notions, or whatever else you please to call them, which a man observes and is conscious to himself he has in his mind; and the ways whereby the understanding comes to be furnished with them.
>
> *Secondly,* I shall endeavour to show what *knowledge* the understanding hath by those *ideas,* and the certainty, evidence, and extent of it.
>
> *Thirdly,* I shall make some inquiry into the nature and grounds of *faith* or *opinion:* whereby I mean that assent which we give to any proposition as true, of whose truth yet we have no certain knowledge.[13]

Regarding reason as natural revelation, and revelation as natural reason, Locke concluded: "So that he that takes away *reason,* to make way for *revelation,* puts out the light of both, and does much the same as if he would persuade a man to put out his eyes, the better to receive the remote light of an invisible star by a telescope."[14] In his philosophy of religion, Locke, a *deist,* believed that God, after creating his universe with the necessary laws to carry on its orderly operation, refrains from any interference with the functioning of the world. He adhered to the deistic view of natural religion grounded on reason, a transcendent God removed from the universe that he created, and morality. God has provided people with everything necessary for successfully coping with life. "Men have reason to be well satisfied with what God hath thought fit for them, since he has given them . . . whatsoever is necessary for the conveniences of life and information of virtue; and has put within the reach of their discovery, the comfortable provision for this life and the way that leads to a better."[15] Because of his deism and the place it accords reason, some Lockean authorities have identified Locke as a rationalist,[16] but philosophers have traditionally characterized him as the empiricist leader of a long line of British empiricists who accepted his view that all knowledge stems from experience and who rejected Cartesian rationalism.

Seeking to establish that no innate ideas or principles exist in the mind, Locke adduced the following potent arguments:

1. All knowledge derives from experience; hence it is false that "there are in the *understanding* certain *innate principles,* some primary notions, . . . characters, as it were, stamped upon the mind of man, which the soul receives in its very first being and brings into the world with it."[17]

2. General assent or universal assent, the great argument, proves nothing. "If it were true in matter of fact that there were certain truths wherein all mankind agreed, it would not prove them innate, if there can be any other way shown how men may come to that universal agreement, in the things they do consent in, which I presume may be done."[18]

3. *What is, is* and *It is impossible for the same thing to be and not to be* are not universally assented to. "It is evident that all *children* and *idiots* have not the least apprehension or thought of them."[19]

4. Innate ideas are not naturally imprinted on the mind because they are not known to children, idiots, etc. "If therefore *children* and *idiots* have souls, have minds, with those impressions upon them, they must unavoidably perceive them, and necessarily know and assent to these truths; which since they do not, it is evident that there are no such impressions."[20]

5. People do not acquire them when arriving at the age of reason.

6. It is false that reason discovers innate principles, and even if it did, that would not be acceptable proof.

So that to make reason discover those truths thus imprinted is to say that the use of reason discovers to a man what he knew before; and if men those innate, impressed truths originally, and before the use of reason, and yet are always ignorant of them till they come to the use of reason, it is in effect to say that men know and know them not at the same time.[21]

Locke went on to maintain that practical principles or moral principles are not innate either:

1. If the principles of knowledge discussed above cannot be proved as innate, the case is more so with moral principles.

2. Faith and justice are not acknowledged as principles by all men. Justice . . . is a principle which is thought to extend itself to the dens of thieves, and the confederacies of the greatest villains; and they who have gone farthest towards the putting off of humanity itself, keep faith and rules of justice one with another. I grant that outlaws themselves do this one amongst another; but it is without receiving these as the innate laws of nature. They practice them as rules of convenience within their own communities: but it is impossible to conceive that he embraces justice as a practical principle who acts fairly with his fellow-highwayman, and at the same

time plunders or kills the next honest man he meets with.[22]

3. Moral rules need a proof, *ergo* they are not innate.

4. Virtue is generally approved, not because it is innate but because it is believed to be true, just, and good.

5. Men's actions prove that the rule of virtue is not their internal principle.

6. Conscience is no proof of any innate moral rule. Conscience, as internal obligation, will not suffice as an explanation of innate moral principles because others also may come to be of the same mind, from their education, company, and customs of their country; which *persuasion, however got, will serve to set conscience on work,* which is nothing else but our own opinion or judgment of the moral rectitude or pravity of our own actions. And if conscience be a proof of innate principle, contraries may be innate principles: since some men, with the same bent of conscience, prosecute what others avoid.[23]

There are instances of persons practicing enormities without remorse.

7. People have contrary practical or moral principles.

8. Entire nations reject a number of moral principles.

9. Whatever practical rule or moral principle is anywhere generally permitted to be broken cannot be accepted as innate.

10. Those who subscribe to innate moral principles fail to state precisely what they are.

It will be recalled that Descartes referred to the idea of God as an innate idea, but this assertion was repudiated by Locke, who pointed out that ideas of God vary with different persons. Locke went further; he argued that the idea of substance, that is, the nature or character of ultimate reality, is not innate since ideas themselves are not innate but are derived from experience. Inasmuch as ideas are not innate, neither can propositions be so regarded.

Some *ideas* forwardly offer themselves to all men's understanding; some sorts of truths result from any *ideas,* as soon as the mind puts them into propositions; other truths require a train of *ideas* placed in order, a due comparing of them, and deductions made with attention, before they can be discovered and assented to. Some of the first sort, because of their general and easy reception, have been mistaken for innate; but the truth is, *ideas* and notions are no more born with us than arts and sciences, though some of them indeed offer themselves to our faculties more readily than others and therefore are more generally received, though that too be according as the organs of our bodies and powers of our minds happen to be employed.[24]

Thus the differences in the ideas of different people must be attributed to variations in the application of their senses or faculties, that is, to differences in their experience.

II *Leibniz and Locke*

In Gerhart's seven-volume *Die philosophischen Schriften von G. W. Leibniz* (The Philosophical Writings of G. W. Leibniz), the fifth volume is devoted to Leibniz's refutation of Locke, a volume that has been translated into English as *New Essays concerning Human Understanding.* Leibniz's *New Essays* were prompted by Locke's *Essay concerning Human Understanding.* Having read Locke's *Essay,* Leibniz sent a series of short critical papers to him, but to no avail. Leibniz apparently expected Locke to take the critical comments into consideration in a later edition, but when virtually no attention was accorded them, Leibniz set himself the task of publishing his own *New Essays concerning Human Understanding.* In deference to Locke, however, he delayed publication in the expectation of a new French edition of Locke's work. When Locke died in 1704, the fourth edition of his *Essay* failed to acknowledge Leibniz's criticism, and Leibniz's *New Essays* remained unpublished until 1765, approximately a half century after the death of its author and approximately sixty years after Locke's death. The book, intended as a defense of Cartesianism, was published in French in 1765 as *Nouveaux essais sur l'entendement humain.*

Access to Locke's *Essay* was gained by Leibniz through the French translation of the work, which initially appeared in abstract form in 1688 in Jean Le Clerc's *Bibliothèque universelle,* and through the fourth edition published by Pierre Coste in 1700. Leibniz's criticisms reached Locke through Thomas Burnett, with whom Leibniz was in correspondence. In a letter to Burnett (July, 1697), Leibniz wrote:

"What I sent you of my reflections upon the important book of Locke is entirely at your disposal, and you can communicate it to whomever it seems good to you; and if it falls into his hands, or those of his friends, so much the better; for that will give him an opportunity to instruct us and to clear up the matter."

The letters of Leibniz were to no avail, for Locke either ignored them or dismissed the remarks with the comment that he did not sufficiently understand them. Following the death of Locke, Leibniz wrote Burnett (May 26, 1706) that "the death of Locke has taken away my desire to publish my remarks upon his works. I prefer now to publish my thoughts independently of those of another."

Plato's Reminiscences or Aristotle's Tabula Rasa *(Blank Tablet).* As Leibniz viewed the issue of innate ideas, it seemed to him to be a question of siding either with Plato, who believed in innate knowledge, that is, knowledge gained by the soul in a previous existence, or with Aristotle, who first discussed the mind as a *tabula rasa* ("a clean slate," or "erased tablet"). Locke, who was thoroughly immersed in Aristotelianism at Oxford, favored Aristotle's view that the mind is a *tabula rasa*, a view repugnant to Leibniz, Descartes, and other continental rationalists. Plato's doctrine of reminiscence was more to their liking.

In Locke's *Essay* (Book II) he sought to prove that the mind (or soul) can exist without thinking, a view that ran counter to the Cartesian argument, "I think, therefore I am." Leibniz objected:

> I hold that the soul (and even the body) is never without action, and that the soul is never without some perception: even in dreamless sleep we have a confused and dull sensation of the place where we are; and of other things. . . . Thus [Locke] accepts the *tabula rasa* of Aristotle, rather than the implanted [ideas] of Plato. It is true that we do not come upon thoughts in these most abstract matters, without external sensations, but in the case of these necessary truths, such sensations serve more as a reminder than as a proof; which [proof] must come simply and solely from internal grounds, as those do not sufficiently understand who deal little in demonstration proper.[25]

According to Leibniz, the mind is (as is all reality) an activity. To be is to be active. Ultimate substance is therefore activity. "A substance cannot exist without activity, and . . . there never even exists a body without motion."[26] Body and mind belong to the same reality and function together in a "wonderful pre-established harmony of soul and body."[27] (For Leibniz the entire universe, as known to man, consists of basic elementary units or monads in constant activity, and he referred to reality as *monadic activity*.)

Leibniz maintained that "petite perceptions" exist, which are beyond human sensibility. These unconscious perceptions or "*insensible perceptions* are as eminently useful in Pneumatology [psychology] as are the insensible corpuscles in Physics. . . . Nothing is accomplished all at once, and it is one of my great maxims, and one of the most verified, that *nature makes no leaps:* a maxim which I called the *Law of Continuity*."[28] Furthermore, according to Leibniz, "By virtue of these insensible variations, two individual things cannot be perfectly alike, and they must always differ more than *numero* [in number]: a fact which destroys blank tables of the soul, a soul without thought, a substance without action."[29] In 1888, when

John Dewey was but a young assistant professor of philosophy at the University of Michigan and about to leave for the University of Minnesota, he published a critical exposition on *Leibniz's New Essays concerning Human Understanding* in which he stated that rather than being a critique of Locke, Leibniz's comments actually set forth his own philosophical conclusions. Concerning innate ideas, Dewey remarked:

When, therefore, Locke asks how an innate idea can exist and the soul not be conscious of it, the answer is at hand. The "innate idea" exists as an activity of the soul by which it represents — that is, expresses — some relation of the universe, although we have not yet become conscious of what is contained or enveloped in this activity. To become conscious of the innate idea is to lift it from the sphere of nature to the conscious life of spirit. And thus it is, again, that Leibniz can assert that all ideas whatever proceed from the depths of the soul. It is because it is the very being of the soul as a monad to reflect "from its point of view" the world. In this way Leibniz brings the discussion regarding innate ideas out of the plane of examination into a matter of psychological fact, into a consideration of the essential nature of spirit. An innate idea is now seen to be one of the relations by which the soul reproduces some relation which constitutes the universe of reality, and at the same time realizes its own individual nature. It is one reflection from that spiritual mirror, the soul.[30]

The severest blow, however, that Leibniz dealt to the Lockean attack on innate knowledge was the argument that animals, although possessing the same senses as human beings, nevertheless lack knowledge of a scientific, mathematical, and logical order. Necessary truths (logical and mathematical principles) derive from innate understanding. "Nature has not uselessly given herself the trouble of impressing upon us innate knowledge, since without it there would be no means of attaining actual knowledge of the truths necessary in the demonstrative sciences, and the reasons of facts; and we should possess nothing above the beasts."[31] Inasmuch as animals are devoid of scientific knowledge and yet share all of the senses common to human beings, there must be something in man that is lacking in beasts, namely, innate knowledge or ideas. Consequently Leibniz argued that Locke must be mistaken in reasoning that all knowledge is empirical, derived from experience:

By what means can experience and the senses give ideas? Has the soul windows, does it resemble tablets, is it like wax? It is plain that all who so regard the soul, represent it as at bottom corporeal. You oppose to me this axiom received by the philosophers, *that there is nothing in the soul which does not come from the senses*. But you must except the soul itself and its affections. *Nihil est in intellectu, quod non fuerit in sensu, excipe: nisi ipse intellectus* "There is nothing in the intellect which was not previously in the senses, except the intellect itself"]. Now the soul comprises being, substance, unity, identity, cause, perception, reason, and many other notions which the senses cannot give. This view sufficiently agrees with your author of the Essay [Locke], who seeks the source of a good part of ideas in the spirit's reflection upon its own nature.[32]

Thus Descartes, though he had been dead for approximately half a century, could speak through his champion, the rationalist Leibniz, whose persuasive arguments could be regarded as an effective defense of the Cartesian doctrine of innate ideas.

CHAPTER 4

The Education of Clarke's Son

LOCKE had an intense interest and faith in education, which he deemed responsible for all the good and evil characteristics of mankind. During the period of his exile in Holland, he set forth many ideas on the subject in a number of elaborate letters to a friend, Edward Clarke, who wanted advice about the instruction of his son, Edward Clarke, Jr. In 1693 Locke had the letters to Clarke published in *Some Thoughts concerning Education*. However, before the letters were published, he made countless corrections, emendations, and some revisions. At the time of publication, almost a decade had passed since he had written the first letter of advice to his lifelong friend.

At that time, in 1684, it was not education in general upon which Locke's thoughts were centered. Rather, he limited himself to the problem of educating a single child of wealthy parents. Moreover, Edward Clarke, Jr. lacked scholarship potential as well as any other notable distinction; his lot was that of a typical English gentleman, nothing extraordinary. It was for this reason that Edward Clarke of Chipley, in Somerset, who belonged to the landed gentry, sought pedagogical suggestions applicable to his son's individual needs as an average lad belonging to the squire class.

Like other persons of his station and birth, Clarke, Sr., a gentleman with a sizeable family, was particularly concerned about the education of his eldest son, who was to be his heir. The first of Locke's letters containing the instructional advice requested was dated July 19, 1684, and the suggestions in it had evidently been formulated in order to guide the education of an eight-year-old boy who was distantly related to Locke by marriage. All the letters dealt with the comprehensive education of children destined to become gentlemen of the higher social classes, for Locke agreed with the concept prevailing in his time that the education of the common people should be limited to knowledge of the Bible and the practical requirements of their occupations.

(Over two hundred of the letters from Locke to Clarke are in the Nynehead Collection of Edward Charles Ayshford Sanford of Chipley. Others are preserved in the British Museum. Clarke's letters to Locke, the property of the Earl of Lovelace, are in the Lovelace Collection. In 1927 Benjamin Rand assembled approximately 375 letters between Locke and Clarke in his edited work, *The Correspondence of John Locke and Edward Clarke.*)

I *Objectives and Principles of Education*

The objective of education for a young man as Locke viewed it was the achievement of life's most desirable state, namely, that of "a sound mind in a sound body."[1] According to Locke, "He whose mind directs not wisely will never take the right way; and he whose body fails his mind will never be able to march in it."[2] A person is good and useful (or evil and shiftless) owing to his education, an education including even those virtually "insensible impressions" of early childhood with their lasting consequences.

However, in educating a child, one must be on his guard lest he produce the result opposite to the desired one, for "there it is, as in the fountains of some rivers, where a gentle application of the hand turns the flexible waters into channels that make them take quite contrary courses; and by this little impression given them at the source they come to arrive at places quite distant and opposite."[3] The mind of a child is as malleable as water, and as easily turned in any direction.

The Role of the Body. Physical health is a paramount prerequisite of happiness. Consequently a strong constitution, one capable of enduring hardships and withstanding fatigue, is to be envied. It is not enough to be born with a good constitution; one must thereafter take care to maintain good health, a goal requiring what may appear to some people to be harsh treatment because it calls for abandoning "cockering and tenderness," which weaken or spoil a child, and for applying instead more severe measures such as keeping a child from wearing too much clothing. Let the child become gradually accustomed to the cold, for, as Locke noted, the body can adapt to the cold as does the face. " 'Tis use alone hardens it, and makes it more able to endure the cold."[4] Thus the Greek Scythian who went about naked in the winter replied to those who expressed their amazement:

"How can you endure your face exposed to the sharp winter air? . . . Because it is used to it."[5] Suggesting that people should go without hats for a while and from time to time discard other unnecessary apparel, Locke observed: "There is nothing more certain than that our bodies will be brought to bear anything and be reconciled to any hardship, if from the beginning it be by constant [degrees] made familiar."[6] He made some extraordinary recommendations — for example, that the feet be washed nightly in cold water and that perforated shoes be worn that would allow the water to enter as one walks through marshes. Going barefoot would be quite beneficial, and, just as a person learns that he does not need gloves in cold weather, he could learn to get along without shoes. "And what is it, I pray, that makes this great difference between the hands and the feet, but only custom?"[7] If from infancy an adult had always worn gloves, he would find himself unable to endure the cold without them. However, he said, all this advice must be implemented gradually.

Begin first in the spring with lukewarm water, and so colder and colder every night till in a few days you come to perfectly cold water, and so continue. For it is to be observed in this and all other alterations from our ordinary way of living, the change must be made by gentle and insensible degrees; and so we may bring our bodies to any thing without pain and without danger.[8]

Curiosity and Its Cultivation. Locke wrote Clarke his firm conviction that curiosity is not a habit to be stifled but an "appetite after knowledge"; hence it is to be encouraged. As nature's instrument for learning, curiosity must not be regarded as a nuisance, but rather must be welcomed as a "busy inquisitiveness" that prevents children from becoming "dull and useless creatures."[9]

Consequently, appropriate methods should be utilized in order to stimulate and reinforce in children a vigorous inquisitiveness or lively curiosity. Locke made the following suggestions:

Not to check or discountenance any inquiries he may make, or suffer them to be laughed at; but to answer all his questions and explain matters he desires to know, so as to make them as much intelligible to him, as suits the capacity of his age and knowledge. But confound not this understanding with explications or notions that are above it, or with the variety or number of things that are not to his present purpose. Mark what it is he aims at in the

question, and when you have informed and satisfied him in that, you shall
see how his thoughts will proceed on to other things, and how by fit answers
to his enquiries he may be led on farther than perhaps you could imagine.[10]

Contrary to the views of many, children actually delight in, and are
pleased with, knowledge, particularly when they come to see that
their questions command respect and that their desire for knowledge
is encouraged and regarded as commendable. Adult attempts to in-
hibit the child's natural curiosity will only impel him to abandon the
search for knowledge, to participate overmuch in "silly play," and to
idle his time away in trifling activity. The failure to treat their
questions with kindness and respect deprives children of the feelings
of success and satisfaction which could motivate them to persist in
beneficial learning experiences.

Locke suggested further:

> To this serious answering their questions, and informing their understand-
> ings in what they desire, as if it were a matter that needed it, should be
> added some ways of commendation. Let others whom they esteem be told
> before their faces of the knowledge they have in such and such things; and
> since we are all even from our cradles vain, and proud creatures, let their
> vanity be flattered with things that will do them good; and let their pride set
> them to work on something which may turn to their advantage.[11]

It was Locke's conviction that such procedures would not only
stimulate learning but also make it feasible for the young learner to
teach his siblings and other companions.

These suggestions were accompanied by an admonition: "As
children's enquiries are not to be slighted, so also great care is to be
taken, that they never receive deceitful and deluding answers."[12]
Children are sensitive to being slighted and readily perceive decep-
tion, which contributes merely to their learning from adults "the
trick of neglect, dissimulation, and falsehood." Especially with
children is veracity indispensable. "Since if we play false with them,
we not only deceive their expectation, and hinder their knowledge,
but corrupt their innocence, and teach them the worst of vices."[13]
Children are like travelers sojourning in a strange new country of
which they know but little; hence care should be exercised not to
mislead them. Even irrelevant questions should be answered
seriously. To the adult, children's questions may not be significant or

worthy of a reply, but to the inquisitive child raising the issue they are of great moment.

When a new thing comes in their way, children usually ask the common question of a stranger, What is it? Whereby they commonly mean nothing but the name; and therefore to tell them how it is called is usually the proper answer to that demand. The next question usually is, What is it for? And this it should be answered truly and directly: the use of the thing told, and the way explained, how it serves to such a purpose, as far as their capacities can comprehend it; and so of any other circumstances they shall ask about it; not turning them going, till you have given all the satisfaction they are capable of, leading them by the answers into farther questions.[14]

A child's remarks can be more significant than some adults assume, and, in fact, the questions of an untutored child may challenge a thoughtful adult to do some serious cogitating. Often grownups could learn more from children's questions than they could ever learn by passively accepting attitudes and ideas prevailing in the community.

Finally, Locke urged adults to be sincere and truthful when children ask embarrassing questions:

Perhaps it may not, however, be amiss to exercise their curiosity concerning strange and new things in their way, on purpose that they may enquire and be busy to inform themselves about them; and if by chance their curiosity leads them to ask what they should not know, it is a great deal better to tell them plainly, that it is a thing that belongs not to them to know, than to pop them off with a falsehood, or a frivolous answer.[15]

Character Training. Provided a child is amenable to suggestion, a surly trait will eventually disappear. In adults, however, lack of consideration for others is less tolerable, especially in a gentleman. If such a trait in a child does not wear off in time, strict discipline, as in sharp disapproval to shame him out of it, will be required.

Children must be taught respect for their parents, an attitude reflected in their reactions of love, esteem, and fear. A respectful child will not express himself in a manner that he has observed to be unacceptable to a parent.

Be sure to keep up in him the principles of good-nature and kindness, and encourage them as much as you can, by credit, commendation, and other rewards that accompany that state: and when they have taken root in his mind, and are settled there by practice, the ornaments of conversation and the outside of fashionable manner, will come of themselves.[16]

Sadistic tendencies in children ought to be curbed. Some children seem to take delight in tormenting birds and other helpless creatures, and strict measures are necessary to prevent cruel impulses of this kind from becoming habitual. Locke declared that "the custom of tormenting and killing of beasts will by degrees harden their minds even towards men."[17] Long before Freud theorized about misplaced aggression, Locke took cognizance of this personality trait, pointing out that butchers were excluded from sitting on juries in capital cases owing to the aggressive behavior required of them by their occupation. "Children, then, should be taught from the beginning not to destroy any living creature unless it be for the preservation and advantage of some other that is nobler."[18] The world would be a much better place to live in, said Locke, if children were taught to respect all living things — other animals as well as human beings. Consequently the youngest child should be taught to take care of pets, to be kind, tolerant, and diligent in looking after them. Such training should commence from the cradle so that children will learn "to be tender to all sensible creatures, and to spoil or waste nothing at all."[19]

Instruction in Reading. When teaching a child to read, Locke advised, provide him with an appealing book suited to his ability. It must be an engaging book by which he is entertained so that he is in effect being rewarded for making the attempt to read. His delight in reading will be augmented if one discusses the stories with him after he has read them; not only will he enjoy this experience, but it will also make him aware of the utilitarian values in reading. This procedure should be applied very early in his education so that he will never become antagonistic to books as if they were only "impertinent troubles that are good for nothing."[20]

The Lord's Prayer, the Creed, and the Ten Commandments should not be combined with other materials of instruction in reading, but should be taught by rote memory and be made as little troublesome as possible. The child should not be encouraged to read Bible selections merely for the sake of improving his reading ability. Neither pleasure nor the principles of religion can be derived from such practice, and no worse reading exercise can be found.

I grant that the principles of religion are to be drawn from thence, and that they are best also delivered to children in the very words of the scripture. But it is far from this to read through the whole Bible, and that for reading's sake. And what an odd jumble of thoughts must a child have in his head concerning religion, who in his tender years reads all the parts of the Bible indifferently, as the word of God, without any other distinction. I am apt to think, that this, in some men, has been the very reason why they have never had clear and distinct thoughts of it all their life time.[21]

Aesop's Fables is a good choice for practice in reading because it provides not only delightful, entertaining stories for children but also useful moral lessons for adults. For the same reason Locke approved of some Bible stories as materials of reading instruction, such as the stories of Joseph and his brothers, of David and Goliath, of David and Jonathan, and the like, as well as the Golden Rule and other simple moral passages. But he warned against the indiscriminate reading of the Bible from cover to cover before the child has achieved sufficient maturity to insure adequate understanding and appreciation.

The Mastery of Languages. Once the child has mastered the essentials of English, Latin should be his second language. This suggestion was quite reasonable, for in Locke's time Latin was the principal language of educated people throughout Europe. He did not, however, approve of the teaching method used in the grammar schools of his day, but recommended the direct method of instruction:

To trouble the child with no rules of grammar at all, but to have Latin, as English has been, without the perplexity of rules, talked into him. For if you will consider it, Latin is no more unknown to a child, when he comes into the world, than English: and yet he learns English without master, rule, or grammar: and so ought he Latin too, if he had somebody always to talk to him in this language.[22]

He pointed out that a Frenchwoman, without using any rules of grammar, can teach a child to speak and read French in a single year or two. If French women teach their daughters so perfectly with nothing more than "prattle," why cannot the sons of Englishmen be taught Latin in the same manner? Taught in this way, a child would not only be successful but would also be spared the whippings and scoldings which generally accompanied Latin instruction in the grammar schools of England.

If there is no one available who can teach Latin in the manner recommended, another similar though less effective procedure can be used, namely, that of

translating the two languages Latin and English, forwards and backwards, one into another, and that at first out of some Roman author, and by using him to read Latin and nothing else. For the nouns and the formation of the verbs, but more than this I would not have him know of grammar. But the learning of Latin being nothing but the learning of words, a very unpleasant business both to young and old, join as much other real knowledge with it as you can, beginning still with that which is most obvious to the senses; such as the knowledge of minerals, plants, and animals, but more especially trees, their parts and ways of propagation, wherein a great deal may be taught a child, which will not be useless to the man.[23]

Note the "sugar-coated" technique here advocated to counteract the "unpleasant business" of learning Latin vocabulary. Locke also condemned the common practice of requiring students to write themes and verses in Latin. If themes are required as a means of clarifying thoughts and communicating them, the students should at least write them in their native tongue "where they have facility and command of words, and will better see what kind of thoughts they have, when put into their own language."[24] As for Latin, if that is "to be learned, let it be done the easiest way, without toiling and disgusting the mind by so uneasy an employment as that of making speeches joined to it."[25] To force a person to write poetry in Latin who has no interest or talent in any kind of poetry is an unreasonable form of torture and waste of time. Why, Locke asked, would any father want his son to become a poet instead of a useful practical citizen? Poetry, like gambling, was in Locke's opinion an occupation which benefits nobody who can earn a living in any other way.

Locke rejected what was then the common method of learning languages, namely, by rote. "Languages are to be learnt only by reading and talking, and not by scraps of authors got by heart; which when a man's head is stuffed with he has got just furniture of a pedant, and it is the ready way to make him one, than which there is nothing less becoming a gentleman."[26] Often a person who has studied a language by rote makes himself appear ridiculous when he tries to express his meager ideas in the words of great men. If the learner reads and understands passages which express a noble thought and deliberately then commits them to memory, well and good; but to force him to memorize any passage that has been indiscriminately chosen is another matter, a method which results only in "a disgust of their books" and an unpleasant waste of time.

The Value of Arithmetic. A knowledge of Latin, writing, civil law, and arithmetic Locke valued highly.

These three, therefore, the Latin tongue, writing a fair hand, and the general part of the civil law, I would have him perfect in, to which so much geometry as is contained in the six first books of Euclid may be useful; for more than that, perhaps, will but do harm. But as for arithmetic, there is no doing anything without it. It is useful in all the parts of life, and of this he cannot have too much; be sure, therefore, he be made very perfect in all the parts of arithmetic.[27]

Since he was discussing the education of a gentleman, Locke kept in mind the need for skill in arithmetic in keeping accounts of personal income and expenses. A gentleman properly equipped to take care of such financial matters will become aware of difficulties long before they produce disastrous consequences. The young student, therefore, should be given an expense account or allowance and be expected to keep records accounting for all of his expenditures in order to prepare himself for the time when he will have to supervise his estate.

If, therefore, I would have the young gentleman obliged to keep an account, it is not at all to have that way a check upon his expenses (for what his father allows him, he ought to let him be fully master of), but only, that he might be brought early into the custom of doing it. And that that might be made familiar and habitual to him betimes which will be so useful and necessary to be constantly practised the whole course of his life.[28]

For young people one of the best means of developing self-discipline, wrote Locke, is to maintain a regular account of their daily business transactions.

Miscellaneous Disciplines. A good handwriting Locke considered a desirable asset, which he also associated with the ability to draw, inasmuch as there was no photography in his time and skill in drawing was highly prized. A person who wished to communicate his travel experiences could of course write or talk about them, but the results would be much more illuminating if he could also show well-executed pictures of places visited. Locke felt that not every person needs to become a trained professional artist but that everyone should be able to draw well enough to describe things visually as well as verbally, for often a good picture can indeed be worth more than a thousand words.

Locke had a negative reaction to music and poetry in the curriculum — music because of the enormous amount of time and effort usually required if one is to develop even moderate skill, and poetry as a subject of minor significance — and he explained that, although these interests do have value, neverthless "our short lives will not serve us for the attainment of all things; nor can our minds be always intent on something to be learnt."[29]

Recreation is important, and time should be allocated to it. "The weakness of our constitution, both of mind and body, requires that we should be often unbent: and he that will make a good use of any part of his life, must allow a large portion of it to recreation."[30] Recreation is particularly useful for youth as a means of relaxation and enjoyment; for example, after many hours of serious study, the student who does not feel drowsy enough for sleep can benefit immensely from recreational activities.

Unlike music, dancing instruction does not require excessive time, and Locke approved of dancing because it contributes "graceful motions" to all of life, enhances "manliness," and gives children self-confidence. The earlier it is learned the better. "But you must be sure to have a good master, that knows and can teach, what is graceful and becoming, and what gives a freedom and easiness to all the motions of the body."[31] It is better not to learn how to dance at all if the instructor cannot bring about this result in his pupil, "natural unfashionableness being much better than apish, affected postures."[32]

Inasmuch as riding and fencing, in Locke's day, were considered essential interests of men of good breeding Locke commented on these subjects, but he felt that riding skills need not be taught a country gentleman in England unless he be a captain of horse, heading his troop at a muster. As for fencing, it provides healthful exercise, but it is a dangerous sport. Moreover, skill in fencing tends to make a person overconfident so that he becomes excessively sensitive about "points of honour, and slight occasions."[33] Since lack of skill often results in tragic consequences, only persons expert in fencing should participate.

Locke was so convinced that the principles of logic and rhetoric are of very little value in developing a pupil's skills in reasoning or speaking that he firmly excluded those subjects from the curriculum. "I have seldom or never," he wrote, "observed any one to get the skill of reasoning well, or speaking handsomely, by studying those rules which pretend to teach it."[34] Consequently only the basic essentials of logic and rhetoric need to be taught. Spending time on studying the moods and figures of the syllogism will not contribute to right reasoning; in fact, the best approach to learning to reason well is to read Sir Francis Bacon. The best way for the pupil to achieve eloquence is to read the works of Cicero. "Let him read those things that are well writ in English, to perfect his style in the purity of our language."[35]

As for natural philosophy (science), Locke felt that none exists and none may ever emerge. It must be kept in mind that Locke lived in a prescientific era compared with the scientific world of today. He expected more from science than scientists and philosophers now expect from it; that is, he conceived of "natural philosophy" as absolute and certain knowledge of the nature of the material world, and believed that the various views held in his day were mere hypothetical speculations. Furthermore, he was thinking in terms of the study of science for a "gentleman" of his period. Consequently he advocated the writings of Boyle as a most suitable text for a gentleman, and, for any potential gentleman who wished to pursue the matter further, he recommended the works of René Descartes.

According to Locke the study of ethical conduct and virtue should be required of all students as a means of gaining effective control over their impulses through the application of reason. Moral principles are to be inculcated through reasonable praise or reproof until they become fixed in behavior patterns.

To that happy temper of mind I know nothing that contributes so much as the love of praise and commendation, which, therefore, you should, I think, endeavour to instil into him by all the arts imaginable. Make his mind as sensible of credit and shame as may be: and when you have done that, you have put a principle into him which will influence his actions when you are not by.[36]

Locke considered this technique far superior to the imposition of corporal punishment (the rod) for purposes of moral discipline and ethical conduct.

Father-Son Relationships. In a wide-ranging letter to Clarke about his son's education, Locke concluded with admonitions concerning relationships between father and son: "As he grows up . . . talk familiarly with him; nay, ask his advice and consult with him about those things wherein he is capable of understanding."[37] Two objectives will be gained from implementing this rule: (1) "it will put serious considerations into his thoughts, better than any rules or advices you can give him,"[38] and (2) his friendship will be won. Locke felt that the sooner a child is treated as an adult, the sooner he will attain maturity, an end to which occasional serious dialogue between father and son will contribute by elevating the youth's mind above wasteful, trifling preoccupations. The parent who keeps his children at arm's length will thereby only encourage them to persist in childish speech and behavior.

Too many parents, Locke wrote, suppress all signs of affection for their children, treating them coldly, more as strangers than as their own offspring, an utterly wrong attitude, for every father ought to show love and kindness in such family relationships. "Nothing cements and establishes friendship and goodwill so much as confident communication of concernments and affairs."[39] In the absence of a warm relationship and mutual understanding, paternal arrangements or even sacrifices for children will be of little avail. They need dependable friends upon whom they can rely and whom they can consult freely. No father should deprive his son of such a necessary refuge. One sincere expression of friendship is more effective than a hundred rebukes and chidings, and a truly interested, affectionate father will often prevent serious mischief because his son will be close enough to him to follow him as a model. A father who has won his son's friendship will soon see the child coming to him for advice on the basis of mutual respect and confidence.

Locke urged Clarke not to impose parental authority upon his son, but only to provide guidance in the light of a lifetime of experience and always to make allowance for the generation gap, the different views and needs of different generations. "You must not expect his inclinations should be just as yours, nor that at twenty he should have the same thoughts you have at fifty."[40] Young people should be allowed freedom of choice, subject only to reasonable supervision, so that the relationship between father and son will be one in which the child "comes to be more afraid of offending so good a friend, than of losing some part of his future expectation."[41]

This view reflected Locke's faith in the power of education to remake human beings, a faith that youth could readily be molded

into an ideal personality by means of appropriate parental guidance. It was a view consistent with Locke's theory of knowledge as set forth in his *Essay concerning Human Understanding;* and Locke repeated the basic argument in his comments about the education of Clarke's son:

> I have considered him barely as white paper, as a piece of wax, to be moulded and fashioned, and therefore have only touched those heads, which I judged necessary to the breeding of a young gentleman of his condition in general.[42]

Note the reference to the *tabula rasa* mind and also the classic Cartesian analogy comparing the mind with wax to illustrate the way in which knowledge is acquired. Locke's faith in the efficacy of education, especially under the guidance of an excellent teacher (he considered the costs of education to be money "best laid out"), was grounded in his fundamental theory of knowledge.

II   *Discipline and Self-Discipline*

One of the major goals of a good education is self-discipline.

> He that has not mastery over his inclinations, he that knows not how to resist the importunity of present pleasure, or pain, for the sake of what reason tells him, is fit to be done, wants the true principle of virtue and industry, and is in danger never to be good for anything.[43]

The ability to control one's impulses is necessary for happiness and success. Consequently the development of self-discipline is a prime educational objective.

Discipline, however, that curbs the mind and humbles, abases, or breaks the spirit by excessive strictness is to be guarded against because it results in a loss of vigor and industriousness as well as reducing the pupil to a state worse than that with which he began. "Extravagant young fellows, that have liveliness and spirit, could sometimes be set right, and so make able and great men; but dejected minds, timorous and tame, and low spirits are hardly ever to be raised, and very seldom attain anything."[44] Considerable skill is required in order to avoid either extreme, for therein lies the true secret of a good education, namely, in resolving the seeming paradox of maintaining in the pupil an active, free, and easy spirit, while at the same time imposing certain necessary restraints and motivating him to cope with difficult tasks. It is a simple matter, said Locke, to resort to the use of the rod, as is commonly done, but that is the most unsuitable of all methods of education and merely produces a miscarriage of education.

Punishment as an Undesirable Pedagogical Technique. One objection Locke had to corporal punishment was that it results in the opposite of the desired effect.

This kind of punishment tends not at all to the mastery of our natural inclination, of indulging corporal and present pleasure, and the avoiding pain; but rather encourages it, and so strengthens in us that which is the root of all vicious and wrong actions.[45]

In order to root out of a child undesirable traits, not punishment, but shame for misbehaving is the more effective remedy. (Locke was not, of course, aware of the findings of psychiatry, which cautions us that the feeling of intense shame often terminates in a neurosis; however, this does not mean that a sense of shame is never desirable, but only that excessive feelings of this kind can be dangerous.)

Locke rejected any form of discipline calculated to arouse antagonism or an adversary relationship between pupil and teacher. It is the obligation of the latter to foster the child's natural inclination to do good and avoid evil. Whipping a child for failing to measure up to educational requirements will merely engender in him an intense distaste for education. Children come to hate tasks in connection with which they have been whipped, harassed, or teased. "Who is there that would not be disgusted with any innocent recreation, which was indifferent to him, if he should with blows, or ill language, be hauled to it, when he had no mind?"[46] It is only natural for a child so to react. Locke was well aware of the principle of association, long before it became fashionable in British psychology of the nineteenth century. In fact, it was he who coined the term association of ideas. With the principle of association in mind, he observed that "offensive circumstances ordinarily infect innocent things which they are joined with; and the very sight of a cup, wherein anyone uses to take nauseous physic, turns his stomach, so that nothing will relish well out of it, though the cup be never so clean, well-shaped, and of the richest materials."[47]

Slavish disciplinary action merely makes for a slavish temper.

The child submits, and dissembles whilst the fear of the rod hangs over him; but when that is removed, and by being out of sight, he can promise to himself impunity, he gives the greater scope to his natural inclination; which by this way is not at all altered, but on the contrary heightened, and increased in him, and after such restraint breaks out usually with the more violence.[48]

Assume for a moment that intense physical punishment yields an apparently successful outcome; yet the true result is a state more deplorable than the disease the teacher seeks to cure — often the real consequence is a mental and spiritual breakdown. Thus a mischievous or disorderly young person becomes a "low-spirited moped creature: who, however with his unnatural sobriety he please silly people, who commend tame inactive children, because they make no noise, nor give them any trouble; yet, at last he will prove as uncomfortable a thing to his friends, as he will be, all his life, an useless thing to himself and others."[49] Corporal punishment, if used at all, should certainly be restricted to extremely serious and rare occasions.

The Role of Reward. Reward and flattery are equally unhelpful in achieving the desired objective of education — mastery over one's impulses and inclinations.

I say not this, that I would have children always kept from pleasant things that are not injurious to their health. But they should have them only as the consequences of the state of esteem and acceptance they are in with their parents and governors; but never to be offered them as the rewards of this or that particular action that they show an aversion to, or which they would not have done without them.[50]

Locke believed that expressions of approval and disapproval should be used as means of control in dealing with unruly youngsters.

Though they are not the true principles of virtue (for that is the knowledge of a man's duty, and the satisfaction it is to obey his Maker, in following the dictates of that light he has given him, with the hopes of acceptation and reward), yet it is that which comes nearest to it: and being the testimony and applause that other people's reason gives to virtuous and right actions, is the proper guide and encouragement of children, till they grow able to judge for themselves, and make use of their own reason.[51]

The important thing to do, instead of rewarding or punishing children, is to chart the right course for them to follow and so far as possible to allow them to be unrestrained and perfectly free in their activities, including recreation and folly. What one regards as faults in a child must be taken not as personal faults but as those natural to his age.

If these faults of their age, rather than of the children themselves, were as they should be left only to time and inclination, and riper years to cure, children would escape a great deal of misapplied and useless correction; which either fails to overpower the natural disposition of their childhood, and so, by an effectual familiarity makes correction in other necessary cases of less use; or else, if it be of force to restrain the natural gaiety of that age, it serves only to spoil the temper both of body and mind.[52]

If the boisterousness of children proves unsuited for the situation at the moment, then an authoritative word or glance should suffice, provided the parental authority has been properly established. Nevertheless, the happy, gamesome humor, suited to the child's age and disposition, should neither be curbed nor restrained, but actually encouraged. "The chief art is to make all that they have to do sport and play too."[53]

Natural Bent to Learning: Its Relation to Play. Those things that youths are expected to learn, such as reading, dancing, and acquiring a foreign language, should be taught by engaging their natural inclinations toward them. These subjects should not be imposed on them as if they were burdensome duties or irksome tasks, because then the young people will adopt a negative attitude even though they might otherwise have tolerated or enjoyed them. In order to prove this point all that one need do is to force a child to play with his favorite toy or game each day for a prescribed number of hours and at a given time, and he will soon be weary of it. The same principle holds true of adults. "What they do cheerfully of themselves, do they not presently grow sick of, and can no more endure, as soon as they find it is expected of them as a duty?"[54] It is important to realize that children are people. "Children have as much a mind to show that they are free; that their own good actions come from themselves; that they are absolute and independent as any of the proudest of you grown men."[55] An important pedagogical principle in the light of the above is never to require a child to do even that toward which he is inclined unless he is ready and feels like doing it. Even if he has an interest and natural talent for reading, music, writing, and the like, let him participate in these learning activities when the spirit moves him instead of forcing him when he is not in the mood. If you pressure a child unnecessarily to do what he ordinarily enjoys doing, you will simply succeed in driving his genuine interest into the ground by wearying him of it.

This change of temper should be carefully observed in them, and the favourable seasons of aptitude and inclination be heedfully laid hold of, to set them upon anything. By this means a great deal of time and tiring would be saved: for a child will learn three times as much when he is in tune and inclined to it, in half the time, as he will with double the time and pains, when he goes awkwardly and unwillingly to it.[56]

The skillful teacher waits until the child tires of play before introducing serious lessons adapted to his particular age and capacity. Cleverly handled, learning can be made as enjoyable as play. "If things were ordered right, learning anything they should be taught might be made as much a recreation to their play, as their play is to their learning."[57] The reason is that children like to be active and will be enthusiastic about learning whenever attention is given to the need for novelty and variety which spark their enthusiasm. Both play and learning are experiences requiring diligent application. Locke pointed out that the main difference between play and learning is that play is a completely free, spontaneous activity.

In that which we call play they act at liberty, and employ their pains (whereof you may observe them never sparing) freely, but what they are to learn, they are driven to, called on, compelled. This is that, that at first entrance, balks, and cools them; they want their liberty: get them but to ask their tutors to teach them (as they often do their playfellows), instead of his calling upon them to learn, and they being satisfied that they act as freely in this as they do in other things, they will go on with as much pleasure in it, and it will not differ from their other sports and play.[58]

Motivation. It is freedom that makes ordinary play a source of delight. The sense of freedom will motivate and sustain the child's interest in any task whether it be in formal learning or in recreation.

Emulation is another motivating factor. Under the wise guidance of parents, the eldest child in the family often can become a model for younger siblings to emulate. Children need models who will inspire them to seek higher levels of aspiration and accomplishment.

If the things they see others do, be ordered so, that they be persuaded it is the privilege of the age or condition above theirs; then ambition, and the desire still to get forward, and higher, and to be like those above them, will give them an inclination which will set them on work in a way wherein they will go on with vigour or pleasure, enjoying in it their dearly beloved freedom.[59]

This is the spur that children need, not the discipline of the rod. But Locke warned Clarke that people who are ill-mannered, especially if they are members of the household in regular contact with the children, should never be allowed to serve as models.

Rewards and punishment are generally effective motivating influences. They can be utilized by parents or teachers to control low impulses and evil habits.

The Role of Domination. Locke regarded the desire to dominate others as the root of unwholesome attitudes and habits among children. The desire to control others as a means of self-gratification manifests itself very early in life; it is exemplified in the infant's peevishness, sullenness, crying, and ill humor, even before he can communicate through speech. "They will have their desires submitted to by others; they contend for a ready compliance from all about them, especially those who stand near, or beneath them in age or degree, as soon as they come to consider others with those distinctions."[60]

The thirst for domination also exhibits itself in the possessiveness of children, who want all things they see to become their own possessions, "pleasing themselves with the power which that seems to give them, and the right they thereby have to dispose of them as they please."[61] The same craving for possessions and power among adults is at the root of widespread injustice and contention so disruptive of human life; hence it must be weeded out of the personality at an early age by supplanting it with desirable traits and habits.

Child Training. Locke declared that children must not be given whatever they crave merely because they request it, and especially not if they cry for it. It is quite proper for a child to make his wants known, but altogether improper for him to demand satisfaction. When children are hungry, for example, they can mention it, and the parent naturally will provide suitable food, "but they must leave it to the choice and ordering of their parents, what they think properest for them, and how much; and must not be permitted to choose for themselves, and say, I would have wine, or white bread: the very naming of it should make them lose it."[62]

The foregoing rule applies to natural needs only, not to fanciful desires and impulsive whims which should never be heeded by parents or even mentioned by children. Young children guided in this way will learn to control their impulses promptly when they occur and before they can develop into potent habitual reactions difficult to reject or redirect. Not that Locke was recommending the inhumane and imprudent practice of depriving children of everything that delights them, "but they should not have the liberty to carve or crave anything to themselves. They should exercise themselves to keep their desires under, and be content in the want of what they wished for."[63] Every person supervising children should observe their attitudes and behavior carefully, rewarding them for the display of modesty and temperance, but all rewards given should be suitable for them and acceptable to them. Rewards should not be accompanied by explanations as to why they are being conferred, nor should they be the end result of hard bargaining; they should be given as natural consequences of approved behavior. A child who has to bargain with parents about a reward for his achievements will lose respect and love for them, for he will realize that he can easily get the same reward from other people without such difficulty.

The earlier children are taught that they must restrain their desires, the more readily will self-control become habitual. As they mature and acquire discretion, they should be given more freedom to make their own decisions so that they will form behavior patterns governed by reason instead of emotions. When they ask reasonable questions, they should receive courteous attention and appropriate answers.

But, as they should never be heard when they speak for anything they would have, unless it be first proposed to them; so they should always be heard and fairly and kindly answered, when they ask after anything they would know, and desire to be informed about. Curiosity should be as carefully cherished in children, as appetite suppressed.[64]

Children often, and siblings most often, confront each other in a contest of wills in order to win prestige and influence over their peers. They must be taught to give up unwholesome rivalry of this kind and instead to treat each other with deference and civility. They will soon realize that consideration for others can win their respect without any loss of prestige.

Parents must not side with a child when he seeks revenge against others for an insult or injury. Frequently the child will complain about his companions as a means of obtaining parental assistance in punishing them. Children who are assisted by parents in such tactics tend to become overdependent and weak-spirited. It is far preferable for them to endure injury inflicted by others, for in this way they will develop strength of character; at the same time, however, insults and insolent behavior must be reproved in the presence of the injured child when it is observed firsthand by the parent. At least the parent should reprove the offender in private, seeing to it that he apologizes and offers concessions to the injured party. In so doing the offender may appear to be acting on his own volition in order that his apology may be kindly received, amends cheerfully made, and mutual respect and love restored between the quarreling children.

Locke's belief in a stoical philosophy of life impelled him to recommend teaching children to part readily with their possessions, sharing them freely with companions. They will find out from life experience that the most liberal person is the one who has gained the most and also has won respect and "commendation to boot, and they will quickly learn to practise it."[65] A single experience proving this point will be more effective than learning a score of rules about good manners, rules that merely perplex and encumber the child.

Destructiveness and Mischief. Children are not born vandals who delight in wanton destruction, nor mischief-makers who get pleasure out of inflicting pain. They learn these despicable reactions and personality traits from other people in the community.

People teach children to strike, and laugh when they hurt or if harm come to others; and they have the examples of most people about them to confirm them in it. So by fashion and opinion, it comes to be a pleasure, which in itself neither is nor can be any.[66]

Parents should remedy such perverse tendencies by implanting in place of them the more natural dispositions of tolerance and compassion. When a child meets with an accident at play or other mishaps, and at times even though the injury is rather serious, parents should disregard such matters within reasonable limits and thereby indicate that they expect the child to endure hardships with stoical indifference.

Teachers should by their own conduct serve as models for children to emulate, displaying constructive attitudes and habits, consideration for the rights of others, and fortitude in the face of adversity.

Pedagogical Principles. Locke formulated the following rules as important principles of instruction: (1) Never permit learning to become a burden but make it a kind of recreation. (2) Never require the child to learn two things at the same time or expect him to master two parts of an action simultaneously (unless their separation is impossible). (3) Do not give him too much material to learn at one sitting. (4) See to it that he does not merely abstain from vice, but acts positively in accordance with the dictates of reason and virtue.

Procedures to Discipline Crying Children. Locke discussed the reasons why the unpleasant, boisterous emotional reaction of crying should not be tolerated. Children cry either because they are insolent and stubborn and wish to obtain control over other people in this way or because they have become too soft or weak to endure pain and misfortune. In neither case should crying be encouraged or even permitted.

When aggressive, domineering children indulge in this emotional behavior to get whatever they want, punishment, however, is not the proper remedy, for it will only intensify their antagonistic feelings.

The restraints and punishments laid on children are all misapplied and lost, as far as they do not prevail over their wills, teach them to submit their passions, and make their minds supple and pliant to what their parents' reasons advise them now, or their own reasons shall hereafter. But if, in anything wherein they are crossed, they may be suffered to go away crying, they confirm themselves in their desires, and part with a declaration of their right, and a resolution to satisfy them the first opportunity.[67]

Corporal punishment per se is an extremely ineffective measure, since it may control their bodies but not their minds. "Without this, the beating of children is but a passionate tyranny over them: and it is mere cruelty, and not correction, to put their bodies in pain, without doing their minds any good."[68] Children are not mere animals; hence physical punishment does not suffice unless their minds are responsive.

For if, whenever they are chastised, it were done thus without passion, but soberly and effectually too, laying on the blows and smart, not all at once, but slowly, with reasoning between, and with observation how it wrought, and stopping when it had made them pliant, penitent, and yielding; they would seldom need the like punishment again, being made careful to avoid the fault that deserved it.[69]

Since punishment in the heat of anger does not reach the mind, it is a futile procedure. The preferable course of action is to repress the

child's outburst with a sharp look of positive command and to punish
him only if this method or other diversionary tactics, such as ridicule,
do not suffice. "For it proceeding from pride, obstinacy and
wilfulness, the will, where the fault lies, must be bent, and made to
comply, by a rigour sufficient to subdue it."[70] But even then the
parent should take into consideration all the circumstances and act
prudently in view of the child's age and state of mind.

Children who break out into tears whenever they encounter the
slightest hardship or disappointment deserve understanding and
compassion, but must not be pitied or overprotected. On the contrary, they must be taught to endure reverses stoically, face
challenges courageously, and cease feeling regretful about any consequences except the shameful loss of reputation for deliberate
misbehavior.

What our minds yield not to, makes but a slight impression, and does us but
very little harm; it is the suffering of our spirits that makes and continues the
pain. This brawniness and insensibility of mind is the best armour we can
have against the common evils and accidents of life; and being a temper that
is to be got by exercise and custom, more than any other way, the practice of
it should be begun betimes, and happy is he that is taught it early.[71]

Parents should encourage children to stop crying about lost opportunities and to welcome a second chance to overcome defeats. This
new attitude will soon become habitual with children, who will thus
achieve equanimity and fortitude.

The Importance of History and Geography. Locke gave the
highest priority to the study of history and geography as a means of
discipline and self-discipline because the thorough mastery of these
subjects would equip the student with a clear perspective of world
conditions and an awareness of contemporary social movements and
trends.

Without these two [geography and chronology], history, which is the great
mistress of prudence and civil knowledge; and ought to be the proper study
of a gentleman, or man of business in the world; without geography and
chronology, I say, history will be very ill retained, and very little useful; but
be only a jumble of matters of fact, confusedly heaped together without
order or instruction. It is by these two that the actions of mankind are ranked
into their proper places of times and countries.[72]

These studies should be undertaken as soon as the tutor deems the
child capable of learning them. As a rule even the youngest children

can be taught whatever falls within the scope of their sense experience, especially things they see and readily commit to memory. *The Role of Playthings.* Locke believed in the educational value of play. He discussed this subject in considerable detail. Although children should have all sorts of playthings, they should be permitted to use them only one at a time. Only when the child puts a plaything away should he be allowed another.

This teaches them betimes to be careful of not losing or spoiling the things they have; whereas plenty and variety of playthings in their own keeping makes them wanton and careless, and teaches them from the beginning to be squanderers and wasters.[73]

These apparently minor considerations should not be neglected, for they can become real contributions to the development of learning habits, attitudes, and personality traits.

The Value of Learning a Trade. Although it may at first glance appear to be inconsistent with the calling of a gentleman, the learning of a trade was strongly advocated by Locke. He suggested that in the choice of a trade, the student should consider the degree of skill required and the amount of time needed for training, as well as the intrinsic worth of the trade itself. Training for professions, such as music and painting, not only calls for native talent but also takes so much of the learner's time that he neglects other more useful studies.

Gardening and carpentry are recommended trades owing to their ancillary values, as, for example, opportunities for healthful recreation. Students and other people accustomed to a sedentary life would benefit from learning these trades that involve both physical exercise and mental diversion. Moreover, quite apart from vocational values, anyone who knows how to make things with his own hands will find such avocational activity to be a source of pleasure and delight.

This kind of recreation is not a matter of being idle; in fact, it may require considerable effort to interrupt one's customary activities and fulfill new interests. Even ordinary pastimes, such as card playing, which can be enjoyed by some participants as spontaneous activities, may become more like burdensome labor than recreation for persons who take them too seriously. Any form of recreation is suitable to the extent that it helps the individual relax and feel at ease, and it is all the better if he derives other benefits from it as well. Too many people fail to realize that both enjoyment and utility can be obtained from wisely chosen avocations, and they idle away their spare time on cards, dice, or liquor instead of devoting leisure hours to worthwhile enterprises of any kind, either occupational or recreational.

Allowance being made for idle or jovial conversation, and all fashionable and becoming diversions, . . . a young man will have time enough from his serious and main business to learn almost any trade. And it is want of application, and not of time, that men are not skilful in more arts than one; and an hour a day constantly employed will carry a man in a short time a good deal farther than he can imagine.[74]

Travel as a Learning Experience. Traveling has its advantages that remaining at home cannot furnish. Too often, however, the mistake is made of arranging for the young student to travel in the company of an experienced guide or director who prevents him from learning how to cope with challenging situations and developing into an independent, spirited person capable of standing on his own feet. In particular, the student must not be given extra funds but must learn to manage financial affairs on his own and to live within his prescribed allowance. Independence cannot be acquired if the students'

money and subsistence is managed by another's hand than their own, and they are by that means never put to the trouble to examine the designs, observe the address, and consider the arts, tempers, and inclinations of men, that so they may know how to comport themselves towards them. A little suffering from his own credulity, inadvertency, or passion, will more effectually instruct him than twenty wise lectures. And at least when he begins to subsist as it were of himself it will teach him to be a man the sooner.[75]

A young student who travels abroad would benefit greatly from being apprenticed to a skilled tradesman. (In Holland, for example, he might well be apprenticed to a jeweler.) Besides learning a trade, he will learn another language as well. If he encounters hardships during his apprenticeship, these experiences, too, will contribute to making a man of him. But he should be sent abroad before reaching a marriageable age, for marriage will make it inappropriate for him to serve as an ordinary journeyman.

Remedy for Idleness. Since children have an aversion for idleness, it is not difficult to interest them in various enterprises, but the choice should be wisely guided so that these will consist of useful activities that will prove advantageous to them. To be considered advantageous enough, the activities chosen should meet one of the following criteria: (1) the skill to be developed from the experience must be worth having and (2) the efforts made by the children must make some contribution to their good health.

The Treatment of Children as Rational Persons. Children, even while they are quite young, should be treated as rational human beings, a fact that should not be lost sight of when disciplining them. In conversation or discussion they should be accorded the same respectful attention as grownups.

When I say, therefore, that they must be treated as rational creatures, I mean, that you should make them sensible by the mildness of your carriage, and your composure even in your correction of them, that what you do is reasonable in you, and useful and necessary for them; and that it is not out of caprice, passion, or fancy, that you command or forbid them anything. This they are capable of understanding; and there is no virtue they should be excited to, nor fault they should be kept from, which I do not think they may be convinced of: but it must be by such reasons as their age and understandings are capable of, and those proposed always in a very few and plain words.[76]

Some abstract thoughts, however, are difficult even for mature persons to handle. Parents should not expect children to be capable of reasoning from abstract principles. Complicated discourses or philosophical disputations serve only to confuse the child and therefore should be avoided.

CHAPTER 5

Some Thoughts concerning Education

W RITTEN at the insistence of his friend Edward Clarke and other acquaintances, *Some Thoughts concerning Education,* Locke's major work on education, appeared in 1693. The book, dedicated to Clarke, expounded the same ideas set forth in the letters written to Clarke during the period 1684 to 1691, with refinements and linguistic revisions. It was published anonymously, but the author's identity was soon common knowledge, and Locke endorsed the dedication in the third edition, which appeared two years after the first. By 1705 the book had seen five editions, the fifth published posthumously though revised by Locke himself. As was the case with many of Locke's books, this one also underwent translations into numerous languages, including French, German, Dutch, Swedish, Italian, Spanish, and Czech.

Locke's *Thoughts,* written for the small class of English gentlemen, was destined to have a profound influence during the course of two centuries upon the education of children in all classes of society throughout the Western world. This little classic in its field laid the foundations of faculty psychology, child psychology, and modern experimental psychology and dominated educational philosophy until the mid-nineteenth century. The theories of faculty psychology have been largely rejected by modern psychologists, who deny that the mind consists of distinct powers or faculties and dispute Locke's contention that mathematics, for example, is the best subject to develop the faculty or power of reasoning. (Plato in Bk. VII of the *Republic* expressed a similar idea about geometry as a means of training the intellect to comprehend all other subjects.) But most of Locke's educational theories and suggestions are widely considered to be valid and useful contributions to child psychology.

The following pages reproduce striking passages from Locke's book which state views especially pertinent to education today, accompanied by comments based upon recent investigations and trends. Although his writings were not so polished as those of certain other great philosophers, such as Francis Bacon, Locke's appeal to practical experience and the vigor of his arguments, as illustrated in the quoted passages, contributed greatly to the popularity and lasting influence of this treatise.

I   *Basic Principles of Education*

He whose mind directs not wisely, will never take the right way; and he, whose body is crazy[1] and feeble, will never be able to advance in it.[2] I imagine the minds of children as easily turn'd this or that way, as water itself: And though this be the principal part, and our main care should be about the inside, yet the clay-cottage is not to be neglected.[3]

. . . how requisite a strong constitution, able to endure hardships and fatigue, is to one that will make any figure in the world, is too obvious to need any proof.[4]

The face when we are born, is no less tender than any other part of the body. 'Tis use alone hardens it, and makes it more able to endure the cold.[5]

Habit . . . will help much to preserve him [the child], when he is no longer under his maid's or tutor's eye. This is all I think can be done in the case: For, as years increase, liberty must come with them; and in a great many things he must be trusted to his own conduct, since there cannot always be a guard upon him, except what you have put into his own mind by good principles, and establish'd habits, which is the best and surest, and therefore most to be taken care of. For, from repeated cautions and rules, never so often inculcated, you are not to expect any thing either in this, or any other case, farther than practice has establish'd them into habits.[6]

The masters of the world were bred up with this spare diet; and the young gentlemen of *Rome* felt no want of strength or spirit, because they eat but once a day. Or if it happen'd by chance, that any one could not fast so long as till supper, their only set meal, he took nothing but a bit of dry bread, or at most a few raisins, or some such slight things with it, to stay his stomach. This part of temperance was found . . . necessary for health and business. . . . You cannot imagine of what force custom is; and I impute a great part of our diseases in England, to our eating too much *flesh*, and too little *bread*.[7]

The great thing to be minded in education is, what *habits* you settle; and therefore in this, as all other things, do not begin to make any thing customary, the practice whereof you would not have continue and increase.[8]

The great cordial of nature is *sleep*.[9]

[Early retirement avoids] the unhealthy and unsafe hours of debauchery, which are those of the evenings; and they who keep good hours, seldom are guilty of any great disorders.[10]

As the strength of the body lies chiefly in being able to endure hardships, so also does that of the mind. And the great principle and foundation of all virtue and worth is plac'd in this: That a man is able to *deny himself* his own desires, cross his own inclinations, and purely follow that reason directs as best, tho' the appetite lean the other way.[11]

The difference [resulting from education] lies not in having or not having appetites, but in the power to govern, and deny our selves in them. He that is not us'd to submit his will to the reason of others *when* he is *young*, will scarce hearken to submit to his own reason when he is of an age to make use of it.[12]

Fear and awe ought to give you the first power over their minds, and love and friendship in riper years to hold it.[13]

Comment. Most educators will agree with Locke that a well-rounded education of mind and body is a gradual process of increasing self-direction. Physical factors are inseparable from psychological factors, and the very young child is necessarily dependent upon adult controls and guidance for his growth and development. How much imposed discipline is desirable during the various stages of growth, however, persists as an issue in contemporary education. Some people remain immature all their lives, but numerous investigations have revealed that both physical and mental growth are continuous, that the rate depends to some extent on individual differences, and that social and cultural conditions in the community can retard or advance the process. Locke pioneered in advocating inquiry into the nature of human nature and conduct, the powers of the mind, and the conditions and methods best adapted to fix desirable habits in the physical, moral, and intellectual behavior patterns of the individual.

Locke's faith in the power of education to foster freedom and self-direction of children while helping them to form enduring good habits and attitudes is shared by most parents and teachers today. Many would not agree with his emphasis on the desirability of enduring fatigue and hardship and a Spartan diet to insure rational conduct and self-discipline in adulthood, but at various times Locke supplemented this view and urged that educative experiences be made enjoyable and interesting to the child. Modern educators might prefer to use the terms *interest* and *effort* and restate Locke's ideas with more emphasis on creativity than on endurance, since they feel that the most interesting and enjoyable tasks can also be adequately challenging and effortful.

II   *Discipline: Punishment and Reward*

I am very apt to think that *great severity* of punishment does but very little good, nay, great harm in education; and I believe it will be found that, *caeteris paribus*, those children who have been most *chastis'd*, seldom make the best men. All that I have hitherto contended for, is, that whatsoever *rigor* is necessary, it is more to be us'd, the younger children are; and having by a due application wrought its effect, it is to be relax'd, and chang'd into a milder sort of government.[14]

If the *mind* be curb'd, and *humbled* too much in children; if their spirits be abas'd an *broken* much, by too strict and hand over them, they lose all their vigour and industry, and are in a worse state than the former.[15]

This sort of correction [corporal punishment] naturally breeds an aversion to that which 'tis the tutor's business to create a liking to. How obvious is it to observe, that children come to hate things which were at first acceptable to them, when they find themselves *whipp'd* and *chid*, and teas'd about them? And it is not to be wonder'd at in them, when grown men would not be able to be reconcil'd to any thing by such ways.[16]

If *severity* carr'd to the highest pitch does prevail, and works a cure upon the present unruly distemper, it often brings in the room of it a worse and more dangerous disease, by breaking the mind; and then, in the place of a disorderly young fellow, you have a low spirited moap'd creature . . . who will be all his life . . . useless . . . to himself and others.[17]

Thus, people, to prevail with children to be industrious about their grammar, dancing, or some other such matter, of no great moment to the happiness or usefulness of their lives, by misapply'd *rewards* and *punishments*, sacrifice their virtue, invert the order of their education, and teach them luxury, pride, and covetousness, etc. For in this way, flattering those wrong inclinations which they should restrain and suppress, they lay the foundations of those future vices, which cannot be avoided but by curbing our desires and accustoming them early to submit to reason.[18]

Remove hope and fear, and there is an end of all discipline.[19]

If a child cries for an unwholesome and dangerous fruit, you purchase his quiet by giving him a less hurtful sweet-meat. This perhaps may preserve his health, but spoils his mind, and sets that farther out of order. For here you only change the object, but flatter still his *appetite*, and allow that must be satisfy'd, wherein, as I have shew'd, lies the root of the mischief; and till you bring him to be able to bear a denial of that satisfaction, the child may at present be quiet and orderly, but the disease is not cured.[20]

If you can once get into children a love of credit, and an apprehension of shame and disgrace, you have put into them the true principle, which will constantly work and incline them to the right.[21]

Comment. The motivation of learning and behavior remains one of the most complex problems of education. Certainly modern educators agree with Locke that excessive severity of punishment or contemptuous reproof of children by the teacher tends to arouse their resentment, loss of interest, and destruction of essential self-confidence. If a child holds his teacher in high esteem and receives friendly correction and guidance, he will generally hope and attempt to avoid further disapproval. Often praise of successful achievement sincerely expressed by a respected teacher appeals to the child's "love of credit," in Locke's apt phraseology, and serves as effective motivation of his continued interest and effort.

During the past fifty years numerous investigations have been completed concerning praise and rewards versus blame and punishment as means of motivation of learning and behavior. Many findings have been of limited application or significance, but the majority have tended to confirm the main thrust of Locke's point of view — his conclusion that a friendly relationship between child and teacher is most effective as the basis for extrinsic motivation. However, Locke's disciplinary approach, his repeated insistence on a hardening process and the control of undesirable behavioral tendencies, apparently led him to overemphasize such extrinsic means of motivation as parental approval and to underemphasize the pupil's spontaneous interest in learning and in activities per se, as well as the value of cooperative group attitudes and achievements instead of individual successes and rewards. If service to one's peers, to community, and to humanity become the most potent stimulants of group enterprises, learning activities will be spontaneous and positive with less need for extrinsic discipline or even self-repression. Contemporary trends in psychology and education strike a middle course between Locke's view that natural tendencies should most often be redirected (and the child disciplined in order to form better habits) and Rousseau's view that natural tendencies are good ones which should never be repressed by adult authority or by the pupil's own "apprehension of shame and disgrace."

III   *Repetition and Habit*

First, . . . sometimes children are bid to do things which upon trial they are found not able to do, and had need be taught and exercis'd in before they are requir'd to do them. But it is much easier for a tutor to command than to teach. *Secondly,* Another thing got by it will be this, that by repeating the same action 'till it be grown habitual in them, the performance will not depend on memory or reflection, the concomitant of prudence and age, and not of childhood, but will be natural in them.[22]
1 . . . keep them [children] to the practice of what you would have grow into a habit in them, by kind words, and gentle admonitions, rather than as minding them of what they forget, than by harsh rebukes and chiding, as if they were wilfully guilty. 2. Another thing you are to take care of, is, not to endeavour to settle too many *habits* at once, lest by variety you confound them, and so perfect none.[23]

Comment. Locke's bias in favor of extrinsic discipline and adult authority is clear in these passages on repetition and habit, and he would have welcomed E. L. Thorndike's law of exercise formulated over a half-century ago which states that repetition strengthens the connection between a situation and the learner's response. Thorndike and other psychologists greatly modified the law of exercise, but repetition, though not essential to all important educational experiences, is still believed to be a useful procedure if accompanied by attentive understanding of the meaning and organization of the learning situation. Even for very young children the trend has been against reliance on drill as such — against Locke's recommendation of "performance [that] will not depend on memory or reflection." However, Locke himself often insisted upon the need for clear understanding as a basis for the formation of good habits and the development of mental capacities. Drill would supplement or reinforce activities dependent on "reflection."

IV *Advice to Parents*

If you punish him [the child] for what he sees you practise yourself, he will not think that severity to proceed from kindness in you, careful to amend a fault in him; but will be apt to interpret it [as] the peevishness and arbitrary imperiousness of a father, who, without any ground for it, would deny his son the liberty and pleasures he takes himself. Or if you assume to yourself the liberty you have taken, as a privilege belonging to riper years, to which a child must not aspire, you do but add new force to your example, and recommend the action the more powerfully to him.[24]

[The teacher you select] should himself be well-bred, understanding the ways of carriage and measures of civility in all the variety of persons, times, and places; and keep his pupil, as much as his age requires, constantly to the observation of them.[25]

Good qualities [of such a teacher] are the substantial riches of the mind, but 'tis good breeding sets them off. And he that will be acceptable [as a teacher], must give beauty, as well as strength, to his actions. Solidity, or even usefulness, is not enough: A graceful way and fashion in every thing, is that which gives the ornament and liking. And in most cases, the manner of doing is of more consequence than the thing done; and upon that depends the satisfaction or disgust wherewith it is receiv'd.[26]

[The teacher must know] the world well; the ways, the humours, the follies, the cheats, the faults of the age he is fallen into, and particularly of the country he lives in.[27] . . . The shewing him [the child] the world as really it is, before he comes wholly into it, is one of the best means, I think, to prevent this mischief. He should by degrees be informed of the vices in fashion, and warned of the applications and designs of those who will make it their business to corrupt him. He should be told the arts they use, and the trains they lay; and now and then have set before him the tragical or ridiculous examples of those who are ruining or ruin'd this way.[28]

[The teacher must] fashion the carriage, and form the mind; to settle in his pupil good habits and the principles of virtue and wisdom; to give him by little and little a view of mankind, and work him into a love and imitation of what is excellent and praise-worthy; and, in the prosecution of it, to give him vigour, activity, and industry.[29]

[From our faulty education] we learn not to live, but to dispute; and our education fits us rather for the university than the world.[30] [Children's heads are] stuff'd with a deal of trash, a great part whereof they usually never do ('tis certain they never need to) think on again as long as they live.[31]

The sooner you *treat him* [your son] *as a man*, the sooner he will begin to be one.[32] [Advise him] only as a friend of more experience, . . . with your advice mingle nothing of command or authority.[33] . . . Hearing him in his turn, and using him to reason about what is propos'd, will make the rules go down the easier and sink the deeper, and will give him a liking to study and instruction.[34] . . . [He will tend to] value knowledge, . . . when he sees that it enables him to discourse, and he finds the pleasure and credit of bearing a part in the conversation, and of having his reasons sometimes approv'd and harken'd to.[35] . . . If the *reverence* he owes you be establish'd early, it will always be sacred to him, and it will be as hard for him to resist it as the principles of his nature.[36]

My meaning therefore is not, that children should purposely be made uneasy. This would relish too much of inhumanity and ill nature, and be apt to infect them with it. They should be brought to deny their appetites; and their minds, as well as bodies, be made vigorous, easy, and strong, by the custom of having their inclinations in subjection, and their bodies exercis'd with hardships: But all this, without giving them any mark or apprehension of ill will towards them.[37]

Because there can be no *recreation* without delight, which depends not always on reason, but oftner on fancy, it must be permitted children not only to divert themselves, but to do it after their own fashion, provided it be innocently, and without prejudice to their health; and therefore in this case they should not be deny'd, if they proposed any particular kind of *recreation*.[38]

As to the having and possessing of things, teach them to part with what they have, easily and freely to their friends, and let them find by experience that the most *liberal* has always the most plenty, with esteem and commendation to boot, and they will quickly learn to practise it.[39]

Courage, that makes us bear up against dangers that we fear and evils that we feel, is of great use in an estate, as ours is in this life, expos'd to assaults on all hands: And therefore it is very advisable to get children into this armour as early as we can.[40] . . . [Courage is] the quiet possession of a man's self, and an undisturb'd doing his duty, whatever evil besets, or danger lies in his way.[41] . . . accustom children to those things they are too much afraid of. But here great caution is to be used, that you do not make too much haste, nor attempt this cure too early, for fear lest you increase the mischief instead of remedying it.[42] . . . The softer you find your child is, the more you are to seek occasions, at fit times, thus to harden him. The great art in this is, to begin with what is but very little painful, and to proceed by insensible degrees, when you are playing, and in good humour with him, and speaking well of him: And when you have once got him to think himself made amends for his suffering by the praise is given him for his courage; when he can take a pride in giving such marks of his manliness, and can prefer the reputation of being brave and stout, to the avoiding a little pain, or the shrinking under it, you need not despair . . . to master his timorousness . . . As he grows bigger, he is to be set upon bolder attempts than his natural temper carries him to; and whenever he is observ'd to flinch from what one has reason to think he would come off well in, if he had but courage to undertake, *that* he should be assisted in at first, and by degrees sham'd to, till at last practice has given more assurance, and with it a mastery; which must be rewarded with great praise, and the good opinion of others, for his performance. When by these steps he has got resolution enough not to be deterr'd from what he ought to do, by the apprehension of danger; when fear does not, in sudden or hazardous occurrences, discompose his mind, set his body a-trembling, a nd make him unfit for action, or run away from it, he has then the courage of a rational creature.[43]

This delight they [children] take in *doing of mischief,* whereby I mean spoiling of any thing to no purpose, but more especially the pleasure they take to put any thing in pain, that is capable of it; I cannot persuade my self to be any other than a foreign and introduced disposition, an habit borrowed from custom and conversation . . .[44] they should be taught the contrary usage.[45] . . . Another way to instill sentiments of humanity and to keep them lively in young folks, will be, to accustom them to civility in their language and deportment towards their inferiors and the meaner sort of people, particularly servants.[46]

Lying is so ready and cheap a cover for any miscarriage, and so much in fashion among all sorts of people, that a child can hardly avoid observing the use is made of it on all occasions, and so can scarce be kept without great care from getting into it.[47] . . . Children, afraid to have their faults seen in their naked colours, will, like the rest of the sons of *Adam,* be apt to make excuses.[48] . . . If you would have him in love with ingenuity [candor], and by a constant practice make it habitual to him, you must take care that it never procure him the least inconvenience; but on the contrary, his own confession bringing always with it perfect impunity, should be besides encouraged by some marks of approbation. If his *excuse* be such at any time that you cannot prove it to have any falsehood in it, let it pass for true, and be sure not to show any suspicion of it. Let him keep up his reputation with you as high as is possible; for when once he finds he has lost that, you have lost a great, and your best hold upon him.[49]

Comment. Note Locke's reiteration of his faith in the motivating force of pride (as a result of parental approval and esteem), reward of achievement (as reinforcement of interest and effort), and habit (as behavior conditioning). Note also that Locke failed to condemn the social stratification of his time, referring to servants as a "meaner sort of people."

Highly pertinent to education in our own time, however, are most of these admonitions to parents — a time in which too often some of the highest leaders in the community serve not as models of virtue and good breeding, but as models of chicanery, obscenity, evasion, and defiance of law, polluting the moral atmosphere of present and future generations of children.

Modern psychologists agree with Locke concerning the power of imitation to stimulate among children desirable patterns of life purposes, thinking, and behavior. Imitation is not always a conscious choice on the child's part; it can be either incidental or deliberate. Blind imitation, however, as in drill exercises, was not enough to satisfy Locke. He knew that the best kind of imitation requires understanding of, and respect for, the parent who is serving as a model. The adult model must therefore be a good one, certainly an honorable, alert citizen knowledgeable about "the ways, the humours, the follies, the cheats, the faults of the age . . ." and he must "work" the child "into a love and imitation of what is excellent. . . ."

V *Four Aims of Education: Virtue, Wisdom, Breeding, Learning*

I place virtue as the first and most necessary of those endowments that belong to a man or a gentleman; as absolutely requisite to make him valued and beloved by others, acceptable or tolerable to himself. Without that, I think, he will be happy neither in this nor the other world.[50]

[Wisdom is] a man's managing his business ably and with foresight in this world . . . [51] a good natural temper, application of mind, and experience.[52]

[Good breeding requires us] not to think meanly of ourselves, and not to think meanly of others.[53] . . . First, a disposition of the mind not to offend others; and Secondly, the most acceptable and agreeable way of expressing that disposition. From the one men are called *civil;* from the other *well-fashion'd.*[54]

[Learning should include] languages . . . to be learned only by reading and talking ... . [55] the Latin tongue, writing a fair hand, and the general part of the civil law . . . so much geometry as is contained in the six first books of Euclid . . . arithmetic . . . of this he cannot have too much . . . [56] children may be cozen'd into a knowledge of the letters; be *taught to read,* without perceiving it to be any thing but a sport, and play themselves into that which others are whipp'd for. Children should not have anything like work, or serious, laid on them; neither their minds, nor bodies will bear it. It injures their health; and their being forced and tied down to their books in an age of enmity with all such restraint, has, I doubt not, been the reason, why a great many have hated books and learning all their lives after.[57]

Comment. Locke's four basic aims of education would be acceptable to modern educators, most of whom would probably agree with the order of his priorities. Moral development of children s clearly an urgent need of our time; competence and good judgment in managing individual and civic affairs are essential; self-discipline and respect for others must never be ignored; and practical skills and knowledge must be mastered as tools for successful living.

Locke was in fundamental disagreement with educators who advocated as the *sole means* of education the imparting of subject matter through reading, lecturing, and talking; he proposed instead a new type of disciplinary education that would develop the mental powers of children by means of experience accompanied by straight thinking, habitual self-control, and the performance of socially approved good deeds. He understood Francis Bacon's opposition to the *fantastic learning* of superstition, the fruitless *contentious learning* of Scholastic authority, and the *delicate learning* of mere verbalisms and polished language devoid of significance or reality. He insisted that children must look "into all sorts of knowledge," not to enlarge the amount of information in their possession, but to increase "the powers and activities of the mind." But virtue, moral development, was to be the highest aim. Plato, discussing "the fashion in which men live," defined virtue as a composite of prudence, fortitude, temperance, and justice, to which Locke might have added the theological ideals of faith, hope and charity. In modern education, too, should not all other aims be subservient to this highest aim, the development of moral character?

CHAPTER 6

Lesser Writings on Education

THE lesser educational writings of Locke to be discussed in this chapter are: (1) *Of Study* (1677), a treatise in Locke's *Journal;* (2) *Some Thoughts concerning Reading and Study for a Gentleman* (1703); (3) a letter written (in 1697) by Locke to the Countess of Peterborough (Lady Mordaunt) regarding the education of her son; and (4) *Of the Conduct of the Understanding* (a chapter designed for *An Essay concerning Human Understanding)* which appeared in the *Posthumous Works of Mr. John Locke* in 1706. These writings illuminate further some of Locke's views and include applications to special problems and aspects of education.

1 Of Study

Locke's comments on education in his essay *Of Study* were probably intended, not for the public at large, but for an individual correspondent. Written in France and entered into Locke's *Journal* on March 6, 1677, the essay was reprinted over a half century later in Lord Peter King's *The Life of John Locke with Extracts from His Correspondence, Journals, and Common-Place Books,*[1] from which the excerpts in this chapter have been quoted. (James L. Axtell, who included the essay in his *The Educational Writings of John Locke,*[2] transcribed his copy from Locke's *Journal* and claimed that King's version is somewhat incomplete and inaccurate. Consequently, for the purposes of this discussion, both the King reprint and the Axtell transcription have been consulted.)

Locke opened his essay with the following statements, reiterating a central theme of his educational philosophy that learning should be a pleasurable enterprise.

The end of study is knowledge, and the end of knowledge practice or communication. This true delight is commonly joined with all improvements of knowledge; but when we study only for that end, it is to be considered rather as diversion than business, and so is reckoned among our recreations.[3]

Although the educative process should be enjoyable, its purpose must be a pragmatic one, namely, practice or communication. For this reason knowledge is less important than action. On the other hand, it makes little sense to act without knowledge.

The extent of knowledge or things knowable is so vast, our duration here so short, and the entrance by which the knowledge of things gets into our understanding so narrow, that the time of our whole life would be found too short without the necessary allowances for childhood and old age . . . for the refreshment of our bodies and unavoidable avocations, and in most conditions for the ordinary employment of their callings, which if they neglect, they cannot eat nor live . . . consider how many doubts and difficulties have remained in the minds of the most knowing men after long and studious inquiry; how much . . . they have left undiscovered; . . . we can make little further progress in doing, than we do in knowing, — at least to little purpose; acting without understanding being usually at best but lost labour.[4]

Since the learner does not have sufficient time to learn everything, he must concentrate upon the kinds of subject matter which will be practical from a utilitarian point of view, to the exclusion of marginal or impractical material.

Study Topics To Be Avoided. Among the unnecessary topics or interests which the learner can ignore without loss or regret are the following:

1. "All that maze of words and phrases which have been invented and employed only to instruct and amuse people in the art of disputing."[5]

2. "An aim and desire to know what hath been other men's opinions. Truth needs no recommendation, and error is not mended by it; and in our enquiry after knowledge it as little concerns us what other men have thought as it does one who is to go from Oxford to London to know what scholars walked gently on foot inquiring the way and surveying the country as they went. . . ."[6]

3. "Purity of language, a polished style, or exact criticism in foreign languages."[7]

4. "Antiquity and history, as far as it is designed only to furnish us with story and talk."[8]

5. "Nice questions and remote useless speculations, as where the earthly paradise was, or what fruit it was that was forbidden, where

Lazarus's soul was whilst his body lay dead, or what kind of bodies we shall have at the resurrection, etc."[9]

The last four comments do not apply to scholars who find the relevant subject matter to be part of their field of specialization. For other students, however, in view of the limited time available for study, those topics should not be considered as belonging to the first order of business.

Study Topics of Highest Priority. Locke declared that students should give the highest priority to the following subjects, listed in the order of their importance:

1. Subjects related to religious belief and personal salvation. "Heaven being our great business and interest, the knowledge which may direct us thither is certainly so, too; so that this is without peradventure the study which ought to take up the first and chiefest place in our thoughts."[10]

2. Subjects related to the achievement of happiness in the present life. "The next thing to happiness in the other world is a quiet, prosperous passage through this, which requires a discreet conduct and management of ourselves."[11]

3. Subjects related to a person's life calling or career.

Rules Governing the Time and Manner of Studying. Locke offered practical advice concerning the best time and conditions for studying, including three simple rules

1. Never study soon after eating.

2. Never permit studies to encroach upon your sleep, inasmuch as "sleep is the great balsam of life, and restorative of nature."[12]

3. Take a respite from your studies in case of any indisposition such as a headache or digestive disturbances.

In addition to these rules, Locke advised learners to bear in mind two facts about individual differences: (1) Certain minds and bodies can endure more stress than others. Consequently each person should be cognizant of his physical and mental requirements and limitations. (2) The mind has its own preferences concerning both the nature and the sequence of studies to be pursued. Whenever he is in the proper mood for it, the student should seize the opportunity to study with concentration and enthusiasm.

The Pursuit of Knowledge and Truth. Having chosen a subject to pursue, with the body in fit condition, and the mind suitably disposed toward study, the student can proceed on the basis of the following recommendations:

1. Be prepared to accept the truth wherever you find it.

2. Do not limit your study to mere memorization, but "endeavour to get a clear and true notion of things as they are in themselves,"[13] that is, reason about and think through the material — do not merely recite it.

3. Think abstractly, independently of words.

4. Neither be overly confident nor distrustful of your judgments.

5. Know the limitations of your mind.

6. "Consider what proofs the matter in hand is capable of. . . ." and do not "expect other kind of evidence than the nature of the thing will bear. Where it hath all the proofs that such a matter is capable of, there we ought to acquiesce, and receive it as an established and demonstrated truth."[14]

7. "A great help to the memory, and means to avoid confusion in our thoughts, is to draw out and have frequently before us a scheme of those sciences we employ our studies in, a map, as it were, of the *mundus intelligibilis.*"[15]

8. Study yourself: your own abilities and defects.

II   Some Thoughts Concerning Reading and Study for a Gentleman

In the Preface of his *A Collection of Several Pieces of Mr. John Locke,* published in 1720, Pierre Desmaizeaux noted that a member of a group conversing with Locke was so pleased with the philosopher's comments on the best methods which a gentleman could use in reading and study that he begged Locke to dictate his remarks. Locke complied, the result being *Some Thoughts concerning Reading and Study for a Gentleman,* a manuscript prepared in 1703. The gentleman who made the request has been identified by Lockean scholars as the thirty-six-year-old Roger Clavel of Dorset. The original manuscript, in Samuel Bold's handwriting, is in the British Museum (Sloane MS 4290, f. 11 - 14).

Improvement of the Understanding through Reading. Locke, who considered reading to be a vehicle for the improvement of the understanding, held that reading has two purposes: "first, for our own increase of knowledge; secondly, to enable us to deliver and make out that knowledge to others."[16] The second purpose is at least equal in importance or even holds primacy over the first as the principal purpose of study, because the greatest portion of a person's "business and usefulness in the world is by the influence of what he says, or writes to others."[17]

Unlike the scholar or scientist, the "gentleman" need not become versed in the sciences, for his "proper calling is the service of his country, and so [he] is most properly concerned in moral and political knowledge."[18] Consequently "the studies which more immediately belong to his calling are those which treat of virtues and vices, of civil society and the arts of government, and so will take in also law and history."[19]

By structuring his views so that they were based on the premise that "the extent of our knowledge cannot exceed the extent of our ideas,"[20] Locke remained faithful to the opinions expressed in his *An Essay concerning the Human Understanding*, in which an idea is defined as "whatsoever is the object of the understanding, when a man thinks. I have used it to express whatever is meant by . . . *notion* . . . or whatever it is which the mind can be employed about in thinking."[21]

It is possible that "men of much reading are greatly learned, and but little knowing,"[22] because they fail to exercise their thought processes adequately.

The next step towards the improvement of his understanding must be to observe the connection of these ideas in the propositions which those books hold forth and pretend to teach as truths; which till a man can judge whether they be truths or no his understanding is but little improved, and he does but think and talk after the books that he hath read without having any knowledge thereby.[23]

Still another way for a gentleman to improve his understanding is to become cognizant of the basic premises upon which any reasoning rests, and to observe carefully the relationships joining the various ideas. Having done this, he must see how all the ideas cohere. "This, in short, is right reasoning; and by this way alone true knowledge is to be got by reading and studying."[24] In sum:

When a man by use hath got this faculty of observing and judging of the reasoning and coherence of what he reads, and how it proves what it pretends to teach, he is then, and not till then, in the right way of improving his understanding and enlarging his knowledge by reading.[25]

The Art of Speaking Well. Two requisites in acquiring the art of speaking well are perspicuity (clearness, lucidity) and right reasoning.

Perspicuity consists in the using of proper terms for the ideas or thought which he would have pass from his own mind into that of another man's. 'Tis this that gives them an easy entrance, and 'tis with delight that men hearken to those whom they easily understand; whereas what is obscurely said, dying as it is spoken, is usually not only lost, but creates a prejudice in the hearer as if he that spoke knew not what he said, or was afraid to have it understood.[26]

One way of gaining this ability is to read clearly written books containing a properly selected vocabulary.

Perspicuity alone will not suffice, for correct reasoning is also necessary. Perspicuity without correct reasoning exposes the speaker to criticism.

Subjects for Study. For moral acumen, reading the New Testament (morality as found in the Gospels, the moral injunctions of Jesus) is without peer. Politics, the art of government, is best acquired from experience and history, particularly that of one's own nation, but law is a useful subject to study through reading. Chronology and geography are essential subjects for a reading list (books on travel may be included with those on geography).

For the sake of conducting himself well, a gentleman serving in government or even as a private citizen should become conversant with psychology. In Locke's time, what is today known as psychology derived principally from experience.

To fit a gentleman for the conduct of himself, whether as a private man or as interested in the government of his country, nothing can be more necessary than the knowledge of men; which, though it be to be had chiefly from experience, and next to that from a judicious reading of history, yet there are books which of purpose treat of human nature, which help to give an insight into it. Such are those treating of the passions and how they are moved.[27]

As an afterthought, Locke noted that dictionaries of all sorts should be well stocked in a gentleman's library. Among such dictionaries should be, in addition to the ordinary type, a glossary, a thesaurus, a geographical dictionary, and specialized ones such as those treating the various sciences.

Finally, one's reading should provide delight and diversion. Books in the category of recreation include plays, poetry, fiction, and the like, but "no writings can be pleasant which have not *Nature* at the bottom, and are not drawn after her copy."[28]

III   *Advice for the Countess of Peterborough*

In 1697 Locke drafted a letter to the Countess of Peterborough. (The manuscript, Locke c. 24, f. 196 - 97, is in the Bodleian Library,

Oxford University.) The letter, *Education* ($\frac{97}{A}$) *to the Countesse of Peterborow,* written in Locke's hand, was in response to a request by Lady Mordaunt. The earl and countess of Peterborough, Charles and Carey Mordaunt, were well known to Locke, who visited with them frequently on their estate at Parson's Green following his return from Holland to England in 1689. They wanted his advice concerning the education of their first son, John, who was about to leave for school, probably Westminster School (Locke's alma mater). The young man matriculated at Oxford University on December 7, 1699, at the age of eighteen.

Locke's letter explained his view of education as a gradual process of mental self-discipline. In answer to the question, When should a person fend for himself and be liberated from his teacher? Locke answered: "When a man knows the trends, sees the method, and has got an entrance into any of the sciences, it will be time then to depend upon himself, rely upon his own understanding, and exercise his own faculties which is the only way to improvement and mastery."[29] However, in those areas "where the studies are in themselves knotty and hard, there the tutor's help is longer useful and to be left of by degrees, reserving that assistance only for difficult cases."[30]

For particular studies, Locke reiterated his previous advice to study history (beginning with Livy's *History*), chronology, geography, and morality.

With the reading of history I think the study of morality should be joined. I mean not the ethics of the Schools fitted to dispute, but such as Tully [Cicero] in his *Offices,* Puffendorf *De Officio Hominis et Civis,* [and] *De Jure Naturali et Gentium,* and Aristotle, and above all the New Testament teaches wherein a man may learn how to live, which is the business of ethics, and not how to define and distinguish and dispute about the names of virtues and vices.[31]

Politics, genuine or true politics, Locke regarded as an aspect of moral philosophy, that is, "the art of conducting men right in society and supporting a community amongst its neighbors."[32] With this in mind, it is preferable to begin with the study of Aristotle's works. In due time, one may investigate anatomy, natural philosophy, and chemistry, beginning preferably with anatomy because its practical function is readily evident. A person should study first those sciences which relate most closely to the senses, then by degrees proceed to the more abstract areas of knowledge.

IV Of The Conduct of the Understanding

Of the Conduct of the Understanding, though published as a separate treatise, was not so intended by Locke, who prepared it initially as an addition to a new edition of his *An Essay concerning Human Understanding*. "I have lately got leisure to think of some additions to my book, against the next edition," wrote Locke in a letter to William Molyneux,

and within these few days have fallen upon a subject that I know not how far it will lead me. I have written several pages on it; but the matter, the farther I go, opens the more upon me, and I cannot yet get sight of any end of it. The title of the chapter will be "Of the Conduct of the Understanding," which, if I shall pursue as far as I imagine it will reach, and as it deserves, will, I conclude, make the largest chapter of my "Essay."[33]

The fourth edition of the *Essay* was published without *Of the Conduct of the Understanding*, which appeared posthumously along with the publisher's apology in a volume titled *Posthumous Works of Mr. Locke* in 1706. Though edited anonymously, it appears to be the editorial effort of Peter King, Locke's cousin. The editorial comment states:

For the greatest part they [the treatises] received not the author's last hand, being in a great measure little more than sudden views, intended to be afterwards revised and farther looked into, but by sickness, intervention of business, or preferable enquiries, happened to be thrust aside, and so lay neglected.[34]

Consequently it is not a finished book with which we are dealing, but an accumulation of notes to form the basis of an essay. Furthermore the notes are at times repetitious and the work as a whole fails to cohere well. Nevertheless, as H. R. Fox-Bourne (a biographer of Locke), so aptly phrased it: "But the incoherence almost enhances the value of the work to us, if not as a scientific treatise, as an index to the modest, earnest temper in which Locke prepared to give his last message to the world as an apostle of truth. Thus 'The Conduct of the Understanding' forms a very eloquent and pathetic sequel to some of his writings as well."[35] Furthermore, various sentences in this irregular and incomplete treatise were written too hastily without Locke's customary precision and force. "These drawbacks, however," wrote Thomas Fowler, "are of comparatively little importance, as the meaning is almost always clear, and the terse brevity of the book as a whole, as well as the many racy passages in which it abounds, offer ample amends to the reader for the tediousness of some few sections."[36] Analyzing the treatise, Fowler commented:

What is specially remarkable in the mode of handling logical questions in this treatise is the emphasis laid on what may be called the moral causes of fallacious reasoning: prejudice, haste, mental indolence, over-regard for authority, love of antiquity or novelty, self-sufficiency, despondency, and the various other conditions of mind which are quite as effective in barring the way to truth as any sophisms, however skilful, which others may attempt to impose upon us.[37]

Some Lockean scholars, for example, William Boyd,[38] consider Locke's *Conduct of the Understanding* second in importance only to *Some Thoughts concerning Education* as a source of information concerning his educational theory.

Analysis of Conduct of the Understanding. Opening his treatise with "the last resort a man has recourse to in the conduct of himself is his understanding,"[39] Locke, as other great philosophers from Socrates to Spinoza had done, attached the highest value to the role of reason in human behavior. He set forth a doctrine of the intellective will, arguing that

though we distinguish the faculties of the mind, and give the supreme command to the will as to an agent, yet the truth is, the man which is the agent determines himself to this or that voluntary action upon some precedent knowledge, or appearance of knowledge, in the understanding. . . . The will itself, how absolute and uncontrollable soever it may be thought, never fails in its obedience to the dictates of the understanding. . . . Ideas and images in men's minds are the invisible powers that constantly govern them.[40]

It is of utmost importance that the understanding be guided onto the right paths in its search for knowledge, since a person's will and actions are dependent upon it.

Three fallacies, or miscarriages of reason as Locke termed them, lead people astray so that they mistake error for truth:

1. The first is of those who seldom reason at all, but do and think according to the example of others, whether parents, neighbours, ministers, or who else they are pleased to make choice of to have an implicit faith in, for the saving of themselves the pains and trouble of thinking and examining for themselves.
2. The second is of those who put passion in the place of reason. . . .

3. The third sort is of those who readily and sincerely follow reason, but, for want of having that which one may call *large, sound, round-about sense,* have not a full view of all that relates to the question and may be of moment to decide it.[41]

Some people restrict their thinking to a single point of view on a subject. Since they read only one-sided opinions, they never develop a well-balanced judgment but remain chained to their biases. One should approach things with an open mind and let reason be his guide. "Every man carries about him a touchstone, if he will make use of it, to distinguish substantial gold from superficial glitterings, truth from appearances. And indeed the use and benefit of this touchstone, which is natural reason, is spoiled and lost only by assumed prejudices, overweening presumption, and narrowing our minds."[42] Reason is the criterion of truth.

I have mentioned mathematics as a way to settle in the mind a habit of reasoning closely and in train. . . . For, in all sorts of reasoning, every single argument should be managed as a mathematical demonstration, the connection and dependence of ideas should be followed till the mind is brought to the source on which it bottoms and observes the coherence all along.[43]

The careful exercise of reason, such as that acquired from a mastery of mathematics, may later be transferred to other areas of knowledge.

This complex question of transfer of training has been investigated by many psychologists. On the basis of their experiments, E. L. Thorndike and R. S. Woodworth, for example, concluded that transfer of training is quite limited.

The mind is . . . a machine for making particular reactions to particular situations. . . .

Improvement in any single mental function need not improve the ability in functions commonly called by the same name. It may injure it.

Improvement in any single mental function rarely brings about equal improvement in any other function, no matter how similar, for the working of every mental function-group is conditioned by the nature of the data in each particular case. . . .

The loss in the efficiency of a function trained with certain data, as we pass to data more and more unlike the first, makes it fair to infer that there is always a point where the loss is complete.[44]

Psychologists today tend to agree that a person cannot train his mind generally by studying any one subject exclusively. However, some transfer of training does occur as in the case of students who learn the value of neatness and accuracy in a particular subject and apply these habits to the study of other subjects.

Habit and Practice. As a pioneer in the psychology of learning, Locke placed great stress on habit and exercise (practice). Merely listening to rules will not suffice; it is necessary to do something if memory is to hold firm. "Practice must settle the habit of doing without reflecting on the rule," observed Locke.

You may as well hope to make a good painter or musician extempore by a lecture and instruction in the arts of music and painting, as a coherent thinker or strict reasoner by a set of rules, showing him wherein right reasoning consists.[45]

Locke's conclusion has been supported by psychologists, such as Edwin R. Guthrie, whose researches have shown that activity must occur for learning to be effective, that "a combination of stimuli which has accompanied a movement will on its recurrence tend to be followed by that movement."[46] It is the movement, not the mere idea, that is conditioned or learned, and "what is learned will be what is done."[47]

The role of habit in learning was underscored by Locke, who asserted that just as physical practice perfects the physique, so mental exercise should produce comparable effects. "As it is in the body, so it is in the mind," said Locke; "practice makes it what it is, and most even of those excellences which are looked on as natural endowments will be found, when examined into more narrowly, to be the product of exercise, and to be raised to that pitch only by repeated actions."[48] At the turn of the twentieth century, Thorndike was arguing in the same vein:

Any response to a situation will, other things being equal, be more strongly connected with the situation in proportion to the number of times it has been connected with the situation and to the average vigor and duration of the connections.[49]

Note the similarity to Locke's statement: "We are born with faculties and powers capable almost of any thing, . . . but it is only the exercise of those powers which gives us ability and skill in any thing, and leads us towards perfection."[50] Not natural capacities but acquired habits make a significant difference.

Reasoning, Understanding, and Education. The object of education according to Locke is not to perfect individuals in a given science but "to open and dispose their minds as may best make them capable of any, when they shall apply themselves to it."[51] Accumulating mere unintegrated facts through reading is insufficient because "reading furnishes the mind only with materials of knowledge; it is thinking makes what we read ours."[52] Accurate thinking requires that ideas be coherently integrated into a systematic whole. Locke subscribed to the coherence theory of truth.

We are of the ruminating kind, and it is not enough to cram ourselves with a great load of collections; unless we chew them over again, they will not give us strength and nourishment. There are indeed in some writers visible instances of deep thoughts, close and acute reasoning, and ideas well pursued. The light these would give, would be of great use, if their readers would observe and imitate them; all the rest at best are but particulars fit to be turned into knowledge, but that can be done only by our own meditation, and examining the reach, force, and coherence of the connection of ideas, so far it is ours; without that, it is but so much loose matter floating in our brain.[53]

What, then, is the business of the understanding? Locke's reply is: "To think of every thing just as it is in itself is the proper business of the understanding."[54] In other words, it is the pursuit of truth, notwithstanding the misuse that some persons put it to. What attitude should a person have toward a given point of view? "First, he must not be in love with any opinion, or wish it to be true, till he knows it to be so, and then he will not need to wish it: for nothing that is false can deserve our good wishes."[55] A great pitfall is found in the "prejudices imbibed from education."[56] A suitable understanding is one that is well supplied with moral and abstract ideas. "To fit the understanding therefore for such reasoning as I have been above speaking of," wrote Locke, "care should be taken to fill it with moral and more abstract ideas."[57]

It is an improper use to employ another person's understanding as one's own. "Till we ourselves see it with our own eyes, and perceive it by our own understandings, we are as much in the dark and as void of knowledge as before."[58] Another common error is that of attempting to impose one's own understanding upon another who does not see things the same way. "It is undoubtedly a wrong use of my understanding to make it the rule and measure of another man's."[59] This abuse of the understanding often occurs in matters pertaining to theology, "that noble study which is every man's duty."[60]

Sometimes people mistakenly assume that merely because they have read a piece of literature they therefore understand it. "The mistake here is," asserted Locke, "that it is usually supposed that, by reading, the author's knowledge is transfused into the reader's understanding; and so it is, but not by bare reading, but by reading and understanding what he writ."[61] Reading per se is not equivalent to understanding. Consequently there are those persons "who aim at knowledge, who with an unwearied industry employ their whole time in books, who scarce allow themselves time to eat or sleep, but read, and read, and read on, but yet make no great advances in real knowledge."[62]

In the final analysis, then, what is correct understanding? According to Locke, "Right understanding consists in the discovery and adherence to truth, and that in the perception of the visible or probable agreement or disagreement of ideas, as they are affirmed and denied one of another."[63] Once again Locke returns to his coherence criterion of truth.

CHAPTER 7

Evaluations and Reactions of Critics

U NQUESTIONABLY one of the most important figures of the seventeenth century, Locke exerted a pervasive influence not only in England, but also in France and America, an influence which spread throughout Western countries in succeeding centuries. The following evaluations and reactions of representative critics may help to explain the reasons for Locke's enormous influence upon the course of educational theory and practice.

I Richard I. Aaron

A leading Lockean scholar, Richard I. Aaron, reviewing the contributions of Locke to his own and subsequent times, summarized Locke's principal achievements succinctly as follows:

His writings secured for posterity the advances which had been made by the most radical and progressive elements of society in the seventeenth century. He consolidated the advanced positions. He did not accept everything which his radical predecessors had taught. Some of their teaching he considered impracticable. But what he saw to be living and important he retained, and in his statement of these matters captured the public ear so completely that it was impossible for his contemporaries and for many subsequent generations to ignore him. Locke's work dominated the English mind in the first half of the eighteenth century, and his influence was almost as great in America and in France.[1]

Aaron concluded that Locke deserved credit for exploring in greater depth philosophical problems that had previously been discussed superficially. Locke set an example to be followed by more profound philosophers: (1) by pointing out how inadequate most of the traditional modes of thinking and teaching were and (2) by questioning many unconfirmed, dubious, or erroneous assumptions which had always been taken for granted. Aaron felt that much of the credit accorded to Hume for such accomplishments should have gone to Locke. Moreover, Locke's contributions embraced a great variety of fields: philosophy; education; religion and religious toleration (if nonpolitical); political theory and institutions; and economics, including money and finance, trade, and agriculture.

II *Hans Aarsleff*

Lamenting the fact that with respect to Locke's writings "we have nothing but a succession of jumbled editions which ultimately go back to the early eighteenth century, without the barest minimum of editorial apparatus, except for scanty indexes,"[2] Hans Aarsleff noted that save for a recent reprint, the latest edition is a century old.

Aarsleff did not admire Locke's literary talents, commenting that his writings "lack the precision, polish, and ordered structure we generally expect in writing of that sort."[3] As noted earlier, Locke himself was unhappy about his belletristic talents, remarking that his *Essay concerning Human Understanding* comprised "incoherent parcels," because his writing was interrupted by extended periods of neglect, and he returned to it only when he was so inclined.

One can only speculate why Locke chose not to allow his name to accompany a number of his writings. Perhaps he was being cautious, or possibly secretive, but Aarsleff is of the belief that Locke's intentions were otherwise. Aarsleff held that Locke,

with all the great men of his century, . . . believed that truth was the result of steady, disinterested search; that it was available to many more than had commonly been imagined, and that the chief obstacle to agreement and peace was controversy and men's self-interested commitment to sectarian belief.[4]

The intent of Locke was to labor passionately for the public good, as God had given him the ability and talent to do. Peace and toleration, the public good, were to be achieved through knowledge of objective truth.

III *Rosalie Colie*

Rosalie Colie asks why, if Locke's thought is "muddled" and his style "awkward," was he so widely read by his contemporaries, many of them philosophers and educated men? Furthermore, he was widely read for a century.

Most people prefer medium to message, and since Locke's medium was relatively attractive, his message was got over by that means. A corollary to this axiom is that if the message is trivial, the medium was relatively attractive, to seem thereby the more significant. Unfortunately, such paradigms of packaging information do not help us much in the case of Locke, whose packaging has often been unfavourably compared to his philosophical contemporaries' skilful manipulations of style. By comparison with the magnificence of Bacon's architectonics and clarity, with the incisive duplicities of Hobbes, and with the witty fluency of Hume, Locke's style can seem as trivial as his thoughts seem to some. Neither medium nor message appears to be worth much ink or paper.[5]

History, however, redeemed Locke, for his works have been studied and valued by men and women everywhere, students and scholars alike.

According to Colie, a perusal of the titles chosen by Locke suggests a lack of confidence. Whereas his titles read: *Some Considerations on the Lowering of Interest, Some Thoughts concerning Education,* or *An Essay concerning Human Understanding,* other writers chose such titles as *Principia Philosophiae, Leviathan,* and *Ethica.* "A shrewd critic might unsympathetically observe that Locke was trying to escape from justified criticism of his work by giving it a title indicating work-in-progress: we know from his own utterances, indeed, that this *was* one of Locke's intentions."[6] Nevertheless, merely attaching a tentative title to a work does not absolve one from being seriously considered and criticized.

How ironic that Locke, who always stressed the importance of care in the use and meaning of words, is himself taken to task by this critic for his careless syntax, his "staccato essay-writing," which is jumpy and awkward!

IV F. W. Garforth

Although he agreed with other critics that Locke's writings are often ungrammatical, F. W. Garforth commented favorably on other aspects of the philosopher's prose.

In general Locke's prose is clear, direct and vigorous. There are differences, of course, in vocabulary from modern English; and the influence of Latin has left its mark on his syntax. Sometimes his sentences seem unduly long; occasionally they are even ungrammatical; but the meaning is rarely obscure. It seems that Locke wrote as he thought . . . adding clause to clause as ideas came into his mind; but his mind was orderly, so too is his prose.[7]

Garforth cited Locke's colorful figures of speech, such as: "shelter himself under your example"; and "we are all a sort of chameleons that still take a tincture from things near us." He assessed Locke's *Some Thoughts concerning Education* not only as an educational classic, but a literary one as well. "Any man," he continued, "who can combine both of these in a single book deserves our respect; he also deserves to be read."[8]

V   *Robert Ulich*

Robert Ulich pointed out that virtually all the basic ideas in *Some Thoughts concerning Education* are not new but quite familiar to the reader of Quintilian, Comenius, and Montaigne.

At the end of the 17th century educational theory was sufficiently ahead of practice to know that encouragement is a better means of motivating than punishment, that character is of higher value than book-learning, and that educational programs will be effective only to the degree to which they are adequate to the individuality of the child.[9]

According to Ulich, the influence of Locke's *Thoughts* is attributable to its precise delineation of the results which the members of England's ruling class desired and expected from education, namely, "gentlemen with respect for moral standards, religion, and convention, with balanced judgment and good common sense, with knowledge helpful for a practical life and decent forms of leisure, and a strong sense for independence as far as their own class was concerned."[10] However, instead of employing private tutors to instruct their children in their own homes, as Locke recommended, the gentlemen of England preferred having their sons attend such prestigious private schools (called public schools in England) as Eton and Harrow. Not convinced by Locke's arguments against traditional classical and humanistic studies, they were contented with these subjects as the core of the curriculum.

VI   *S. J. Curtis and M. E. A. Boultwood*

S. J. Curtis and M. E. A. Boultwood considered Locke's most important original contribution to educational theory to be his advocacy of disciplinary training, that is, procedures to harden both mind and body. They pointed out that Locke may have taken from Aristotle the principle that the immature, growing child must not be protected against physical, mental, and spiritual dangers, but, on the contrary, must become accustomed to them. They regarded as a corollary of this principle Locke's statement that the hardening process would enable the individual child to develop habits of self-control and self-direction.

Curtis and Boultwood attributed Locke's reputation as a great educator more to his *An Essay concerning Human Understanding* than to his treatise on education.

He was a philosopher with a point of view, and because the great minds of Europe respected him to the point of reverence, his unorganized, repetitive *Thoughts* were accepted, even by Rousseau, as new and original. The ideas contained in his collection of letters and in his suggestions for working schools were, in fact, by no means of his own inception. His contribution to education was in the application of his shrewd realist philosophy to the opinions on child training which had been formed by English intelligentsia who welded together Puritan-Comenian ideas and emigré-aristocratic standards. Had Sir William Petty published his later educational ideas they would certainly have been similar to those of Locke, and it must be suspected that Locke gained much from men like Petty and Boyle.[11]

It should be noted, however, that Petty did not publish his later educational ideas, and this argument which detracts from the stature of Locke is itself based on the *argumentum ad ignorantiam* fallacy.

These scholars also criticized Locke for his failure to make his educational proposals part of an overall plan to enhance the welfare of the nation as a whole, not merely that of an elite class. But the members of the elite class at the close of the seventeenth century were themselves interested in a somewhat broader education for their children than the grammar schools offered, and Locke's educational ideas in due time spread among all classes and national programs of education. Furthermore, Locke at times deviated from his own *tabula rasa* theory by acknowledging the existence of innate aptitudes and capacities in individuals. In his *Thoughts* he admitted that there is a "great inequality of parts" among "men of equal education," and that both in the backwoods of America and in the schools of Athens "men of several abilities in the same kind" are produced.

VII *Robert Hebert Quick*

Robert Hebert Quick objected to the inordinate role of reason in Locke's writings, not because reason is unimportant, but rather because overemphasis on this factor subordinates other major elements of the human personality.

It seems to me then that Locke much exaggerates the power of the individual reason for getting at the truth. And to exaggerate the importance of one function of the mind is to unduly diminish the importance of the rest. Thus we find that in Locke's scheme of education little thought is taken for the play of the affections and feelings; and as for the imagination it is treated merely as a source of mischief.[12]

Quick noted that Locke's system of educational theory is based on the premise that the acquisition of true knowledge is accomplished solely through the exercise of reason. Inasmuch as the child is devoid of rational powers, it follows that he is precluded from acquiring knowledge until he reaches an age of sufficient maturity. Education in childhood therefore is limited to training in habit formation. Besides the formation of good habits there is training in physical health, that is, physical education. These Lockean theories were subsequently adopted by Rousseau.

In the most celebrated work which has been affected by the *Thoughts* of Locke, Rousseau's *Émile,* we find childhood treated in a manner altogether different from youth: the child's education is mainly physical, and instruction is not given till the age of twelve. Locke's system on first sight seems very different to this, but there is a deeper connection between the two than is usually observed. We have seen that Locke allowed nothing to be knowledge that was not acquired by the perception of the intellect. But in children the intellectual power is not yet developed; so according to Locke knowledge properly so-called is not within their reach. What then can the educator do for them? He can prepare them for the age of reason in two ways, by caring first for their physical health, second for the formation of good habits.[13]

As Quick reminded us, this advocacy of bodily care and physical exercise was not new with Locke, for the English scholar Sir Thomas Elyot (1490? - 1546), the English schoolmaster Richard Mulcaster (1530? - 1611), and the English poet John Milton (1608 - 1674) had earlier espoused the same regimen.

Quick severely criticized Locke's conception of the human mind as a *tabula rasa:*

No language could bring out more clearly the inferiority of Locke's standpoint to that of later thinkers. He makes little account of our common nature and wishes education to be based upon an estimate of the peculiarities of the individual pupil and of his social needs. And no one with an adequate notion of education could ever compare the young child to "white paper or wax."[14]

As noted above, however, Locke modified his view by accepting the idea of innate aptitudes and capacities.

VIII   F. Andrew Brown

In an article entitled "On Education: John Locke, Christian Wolff, and the 'Moral Weeklies,' "[15] F. Andrew Brown made a number of observations with respect to the educational philosophy of Locke, particularly in the light of its effect on educational theory in Germany. Brown noted that Locke's *Thoughts* did more than capture the French; it enlisted considerable German support. The book was not only translated into French almost immediately after its publication in English; it was reprinted numerous times both in French and in German. There was a French version as early as 1695 (in Amsterdam), a Dutch translation in 1697 - 1698, and a German translation in 1708. The popularity of the book actually increased during the latter half of the eighteenth century.

Brown wrote that, although many of Locke's thoughts expressed in his treatise on education were original, others were verbal expressions of the growing tendency of the time, for Locke was caught up in a *Zeitgeist*. Traditional Latin schools were coming under reform in the late seventeenth century, yielding to the mother tongue. Caught up in this spirit, Locke called for the teaching of the mother tongue and other modern languages. Other reforms espoused by him called for educating people to assume their respective roles in society; making the learning process a vital, natural, and pleasant experience; ascertaining the child's natural temperament and gearing education to it; capitalizing on the child's natural curiosity; enlisting the child's play to pedagogical advantage; emphasizing physical as well as intellectual education; and using all of the child's experiences as a vehicle of education. According to Brown, Locke's contemporaries got from him

their justification for glorifying reason; the power of judgment could be developed gradually as the *tabula rasa* of the mind was exposed under careful guidance to the experience which provided it with the materials of thought. Properly carried out, education meant progress along the pathways of reason; and where reason dwelt, virtue could not be far off. For Locke, virtue, as nearly as he defined it, meant that quality of mind which led an individual to choose the course of action dictated by reason, even where inclination or desire indicated another choice.[16]

Brown credited Locke with restoring to the child, who previously had been considered a mere receptacle into which the teacher would pour his own notions, his status as a person. No longer were children to be treated as thoughtless creatures controllable only by severe punishment; rather, they were to be treated as rational beings who could be disciplined by reasoned persuasion. Locke repeatedly condemned severe deprivation and corporal punishment as futile and repugnant.

Brown also regarded Locke as avant-garde in recommending that virtue be inculcated through the emulation of respected living models and the practice of moral standards rather than by the memorization of rules or precepts. Locke was far ahead of his time in calling for mutual respect between parent and child. The adage "respect your elders" must have the corollary "reverence your son."

Brown's article praised Locke for several other important contributions. Locke was one of the first educators to advocate full exploitation of the child's powers of observation. He insisted upon the necessity for establishing good habits in the earliest years of childhood. Practice and repetition were his bywords for acquiring good habits. He advocated the study of each child's psychological traits, natural endowments, and temperament to provide for individual differences and help him to achieve physical health and mental development. Personality traits were to be carefully considered in the choice of a career. As Brown pointed out, these ideas have a distinctly modern ring to them; they undoubtedly stimulated the thinking of later educators and found their way into educational theory and practice.

IX *Alfred Adler, John B. Watson, and John Dewey*

Three famous thinkers of the twentieth century, namely, Alfred Adler (1870 - 1937), John B. Watson (1878 - 1958), and John Dewey (1859 - 1952), formulated a number of major ideas which seem to be virtually echoes of views expounded by Locke.

It will be recalled that Locke, stoical in outlook, advocated a process of gradual hardening to develop in the child a "sound mind in a sound body." He condemned coddling and overprotection as roots of ill health. The Viennese psychiatrist Adler lent support to

Locke's contention by reporting that people who are overprotected during childhood (usually the youngest in the family) cannot cope with life as adults, because as children they had lacked opportunities to deal with its vicissitudes; their parents had removed all problems from their paths instead of allowing them to deal with life's difficult situations and thereby learn to adapt.

We know that every pampered child becomes a hated child. Our civilization is such that neither society nor the family wishes to continue the pampering process indefinitely. A pampered child is very soon confronted with life's problems. In school he finds himself in a new social institution, with a new social problem. He does not want to work or play with his fellows, for his experience has not prepared him for the communal life of the school. In fact his experiences as lived through at the prototype stage make him afraid of such situations and make him look for more pampering. Now the characteristics of such an individual are not inherited — far from it — for we can deduce them from a knowledge of the nature of his prototype and his goal.[17]

Locke's contention that constant activity of children is a natural means of self-education received confirmation in the researches of Watson, who concluded that "the role of all instinctive activity is to initiate the process of learning."[18] Watson went on to assert that

from the moment of birth the infant when not sleeping is moving almost ceaselessly the arms, hands, legs, eyes, head, and indeed the whole body. Stimulate him in any way and these movements become more frequent and increase in amplitude. . . . It can be maintained from our experimental work on habit that the autonomic system furnishes the restless seeking or avoiding movements of the body as a whole which lead the organism to display the instinctive repertoire out of which habits are composed.[19]

Locke's insistence on learning from experience and on encouraging child activities, especially play activities, as an essential method of growth and development became a central thesis of the so-called "progressive education" movement in this century under the leadership of Dewey, who wrote:

If one attempts to formulate the philosophy of education implicit in the practices of the new education, we may, I think, discover certain common principles amid the variety of progressive schools now existing. To imposition from above is opposed expression and cultivation of individuality; to external discipline is opposed free activity; to learning from texts and teachers, learning through experience; to acquisition of isolated skills and techniques by drill, is opposed acquisition of them as means of attaining ends which make direct vital appeal; to preparation for a more or less remote future is opposed making the most of the opportunities of present life; to static aims and materials is opposed acquaintance with a changing world.[20]

The educational reforms advocated by Locke found receptive ears among great philosophers long before Dewey, as, for example, Baron Christian von Wolff (1679 - 1754) who championed Locke's educational theories in the "Moral Weeklies" (journals published in Germany concerning educational theory, religion, and ethics) two centuries ago.

X   *William Boyd*

William Boyd noted a sharp distinction between Locke's *Of the Conduct of the Understanding* and his *Thoughts*. "The education contemplated in the latter," wrote Boyd, "is quite specific — it is a preparation for a particular kind of life; that contemplated in the former is quite general — it is the preparation of the intellect for any kind of life."[21] Contrasting the two books in still another manner, he said that one approaches the subject objectively, the other, subjectively. "The *Thoughts* states the aim of education in objective terms, as consisting in the acquisition of certain forms of knowledge and skill; the essay *[Of the Conduct of the Understanding]*, in subjective terms, as the training of mental faculties."[22] Locke failed to distinguish the relationship between the two treatises, probably because he was totally unaware that he was offering two different points of view. "The possibility that there might be no faculties of mind capable of a general formal training," asserted Boyd, "certainly never occurred to him, any more than to the innumerable educators, both before and after him, who have uncritically assumed that training faculties and preparing for social functions are alternative expressions for the same fact."[23]

In his *From Locke to Montessori*, Boyd held that the prestige and popularity of Locke's educational writings resulted from his renown as the author of the classic *An Essay concerning Human Understanding*. Without the *Essay* to his credit, doubts arise as to whether Locke would have been widely read and would have had such great influence in the field of education. Commenting on the matter Boyd wrote:

To some extent, no doubt, the attention paid to them *[Some Thoughts concerning Education* and *Conduct of the Understanding]* was due to the great reputation of the *Essay concerning Human Understanding* rather than to their intrinsic merits. But with all their limitations they were worthy of the attention they got; for they had implicit in them a new conception of education which was destined to play almost as great and as varied a part in the development of educational doctrine as the new point of view of the *Essay* in the development of philosophy. The *Essay* made individual experience the central theme of philosophical thought. The *Thoughts concerning Education* treated the individual pupil as the main concern of the educator.[24]

The wave of individualism on which Locke was riding, Boyd noted, was deeply rooted in the growing revolt against authority at the time, culminating in the Revolution of 1688. It was Locke's medical training, wrote Boyd, that gave him the necessary perspective to bring a fresh view to educational theory and to break with the educational traditions of the time, especially those which had become customary in grammar schools during the Renaissance. Locke was viewing the pupil as a physician does his patient, that is, as someone to be treated as an individual in the light of his particular condition and temperament.

XI   *John W. Yolton*

John W. Yolton warned the readers of *Some Thoughts concerning Education* that they will obtain from it a misconception of Locke's educational philosophy unless they keep in mind his purposes in writing the treatise and the situation in which he found himself at the time. According to Yolton,

> In interpreting Locke's *Thoughts concerning Education,* one must always be careful not to blow it up beyond its own proportions. It was a treatise limited to a time and place, and even to a particular child. . . . There are few hints about what Locke would have done differently, were he writing "a just treatise" on education.[25]

Yolton pointed to Locke's own statement that he was offering "only some general views, in reference to the main end, and aims in education, and those designed for a gentleman's son."[26] Moreover, Locke admitted that "there are a thousand other things, that may need consideration; especially if one should take in the various tempers, different inclinations, and particular defaults, that are to be found in children; and prescribe proper remedies."[27] Locke's insistence that education should be tailored to a specific purpose implies that the only effective education is the kind that is individualized. "By ending on the need to particularize discussions on education to specific types of minds and abilities, Locke may be saying in effect that general treatises on education have limited value at best,"[28] commented Yolton. "The most effective approach to education is not through general theories and general rules, but through a careful study of individual persons."[29] Noting that the major goals of education for Locke are to be achieved only through the adaptation of teaching techniques to the pupil's interests, potentialities, and talents, Yolton agreed with this approach and its implications for modern education:

> The tutorial method is especially appropriate just because it provides the context in which the child's tempers and frame of mind can most easily be understood. We today may often forget this simple truth, assuming . . . that the similarities among people provide a sufficient basis for educating in the mass. Locke's remarks on education may still have importance for us if they can remind us of the need to particularize our educational methods.[30]

It was Yolton's opinion that Locke, even though he might not have formulated specific instructional methods which educationists today could implement, promulgated goals that should still be acceptable as a basis for educational procedures and programs. Locke understood and appreciated well the importance of education both for the individual and for society as a whole.

In his *John Locke and the Way of Ideas,* Yolton concluded that Locke had not originally intended to perpetuate discussions about Cartesian metaphysics or to undertake the kind of philosophical analysis traditional among medievalists. Locke was mainly concerned about the moral and theological issues of his time. To quote Yolton:

> If one examines the moral and religious context in which Locke was living at the time of his reflections, it becomes quite clear that one of the traits of the *Essay* which created such an active interest in Locke's contemporaries was the way in which its philosophical doctrines were almost always directly related to the moral and religious disputes of the day. This relevance gave to Locke's work an immediate importance for his readers. What came to fan the flames of controversy and invective was the solutions he proposed to the traditional disputes.[31]

Nevertheless, Locke's solutions to traditional disputes of philosophers only indirectly disturbed his readers, for he emphasized religious and moral issues in a manner agreeable to them, and it was not these issues that posed the main and annoying problems but epistemology, that is, problems about the nature and limits of knowledge, particularly about its genuine or spurious character. The question of knowledge never left Locke; it persisted as a decisive consideration not only in the *Essay* but in all his other writings as well.

XII   *Norman Kemp Smith*

Norman Kemp Smith noted that Locke took over from Descartes the method of rationalism, the doctrine of clear and distinct ideas, but repudiated that great philosopher's theory of innate ideas and his dualism, which sharply divided mind from body.[32] Locke was unable to see how a person could be thought of as existing apart from his body. Adopting Descartes's "trust in reason as exercising supreme sovereignty in all matters of controversy," Locke then reformulated "these doctrines in the manner demanded by the results of the empirical sciences, and especially of Newton's great discoveries."[33] In this way "Locke became the chief channel through which all that could be immediately fruitful in Descartes's teaching came to its own; and it was these parts of Locke's philosophy that alone gained general currency in France."[34] The French accepted Locke à la France, that is, they cut "him to a French pattern, as befitted the rôle assigned to him."[35] Thus Descartes the metaphysician was superseded by Locke the philosopher. With Locke's *Essay* following Newton's *Principia* by four years, one can see why Voltaire in hiss great crusade adopted as his battle cry: "the Newtonian Philosophy and Locke as its Prophet."

Smith commented on the ironic characterization of the modest Locke as Plato's rival:

In the comedy of life, time plays strange tricks with men and affairs. Here we have Locke, the most modest of men, being set on a pedestal as a rival to Plato, or when attacked by his enemies treated as an influence so powerful as to have poisoned the mind of a whole century. That Locke should have lent himself to such apotheosis and attack, is easily understandable as regards his controversial writings — Locke the protagonist of toleration, Locke as standing for constitutional rights and for individual liberty, and for a simplified theology, Locke the educationalist, Locke the opponent of innate ideas. . . . It was natural that the importance of these writings should be overestimated. Just because of their immediate serviceableness, being written to meet contemporary needs, nothing in them was likely to fail of effect.[36]

Locke was the most influential philosopher in Great Britain, and his philosophy also dominated continental Europe, particularly in France, where he displaced that philosophical titan Descartes.

Notes and References

Chapter One

1. Benjamin Rand, *The Correspondence of John Locke and Edward Clarke* (Cambridge, Mass.: Harvard University Press, 1927), p. 1.
2. Lady Masham to Jean Le Clerc, January 12, 1704 - 1705, Remonstrants' Library, Amsterdam.
3. John Locke, *Some Thoughts concerning Education*, rev. ed. (Cambridge: Cambridge University Press, 1884), sec. 40.
4. *Ibid.*
5. Locke to Clarke, February 26, 1691.
6. W. N. Hargreaves-Mawdsley, *Oxford in the Age of John Locke* (Norman, Oklahoma: University of Oklahoma Press, 1973), p. 20.
7. *Some Thoughts concerning Education*, sec. 188.
8. *Ibid.*, sec. 180.
9. *Ibid.*, sec. 184.
10. The verses are found in H. R. Fox-Bourne, *The Life of John Locke*, 2 vols. (London: Henry S. King, 1876), vol. 1, pp. 50 - 52.
11. Fixing the dates for the life of Locke is difficult because two different calendars were in use. Cranston has explained that a difficulty confronts the historian who writes of the period between 1582 and 1752 because two calendars were then employed. Most of the Western States of Continental Europe then used the Gregorian or New Style calendar; England conservatively and Protestantly (for the Gregorian calendar, though accurate, was Papal in origin) stuck to the Julian or Old Style calendar. As Locke corresponded on a considerable scale with continental friends, and spent several years in France and Holland, the disparity of dates according to the two systems of reckoning is bewildering to the student of his life and documents (Maurice Cranston, *John Locke: A Biography* [New York: Macmillan, 1957], p. xii).
12. Quoted in Cranston, *op. cit.*, p. 118.
13. *Ibid.*, p. 119.
14. J. 20, Remonstrants' Library, Amsterdam.
15. Locke to Clarke, b. 4, f. 75, Bodleian Library, Oxford.

Chapter Two

1. See *Some Thoughts concerning Education*, secs. 184 - 86, 188 - 89.
2. Thomas Hobbes, *Leviathan* (1651), pt. 1, chap. 13.
3. Nathanael Culverwel, *The Light of Nature* (1652), chap. 1.
4. Richard Cumberland, *A Treatise of the Laws of Nature* (London, 1727), chap. 1 sec. 4. (John Maxwell's version of Cumberland's original treatise)
5. Benjamin Whichcote, "The Work of Reason," *Select Sermons* (London, 1689).
6. John Locke, *An Essay concerning Human Understanding* (London: J. M. Dent, 1961), bk. 1, chap. 3, sec. 15.
7. *The Reasonablesness of Christianity* (London, 1824), pp. 4 - 5; vol. 6 of *The Works of John Locke*.
8. *An Essay concerning Human Understanding*, bk. 4, chap. 1, sec. 2; chap. 5, sec. 2.
9. *Ibid.*, "The Epistle to the Reader."
10. *Ibid.*, bk. 2, chap. 1, secs. 3 - 4.
11. *Ibid.*, chap. 1, sec. 24.
12. *Ibid.*, chap. 2, sec. 2.
13. *Ibid.*, chap. 8, sec. 8.
14. *Ibid.*, sec. 10.
15. *Ibid.*, chap. 11, sec. 9.
16. *Ibid.*, chap. 23, sec. 1.
17. *Ibid.*, sec. 2.
18. *Ibid.*, sec. 14.
19. *Ibid.*, sec. 15.
20. *Ibid.*, chap. 33, sec. 5.
21. Thomas Hobbes, *Human Nature* (1650), chap. 4, sec. 2.
22. David Hume, *A Treatise of Human Nature* (1739), bk. 1, pt. 4, chap. 6.
23. Edward Stillingfleet. *The Bishop of Worcester's Answer to Mr. Locke's Letter concerning Some Passages Relating to his Essay concerning Human Understanding Mentioned in the Late Discourse in Vindication of the Trinity* (London, 1697), and *The Bishop of Worcester's Answer to Mr. Locke's Second Letter, Wherein His Notion of Ideas Is Proved to Be Inconsistent with Itself and with the Articles of the Christian Faith* (London, 1698).
24. *An Essay concerning Human Understanding*, bk. 4, chap. 4, secs. 1 and 3.
25. *Ibid.*, sec. 3.
26. *Ibid.*, bk. 2, chap. 31, sec. 6.
27. *Ibid.*, bk. 4, chap. 5, sec. 11.
28. *Ibid.*, bk. 3, chap. 11, sec. 16.
29. *Ibid.*, bk. 4, chap. 3, sec. 18.
30. George Berkeley, *Commonplace Book*, in *Works* (Oxford: Clarendon Press, 1901), vol. 1, p. 39.

31. *An Essay concerning Human Understanding*, bk. 3, chap. 5, secs. 2 - 3.

32. *Ibid.*, bk. 2, chap. 21, secs. 41 - 42.

33. *Ibid.*, sec. 43.

34. *Ibid.*

35. *Ibid.*, chap. 20, sec. 2.

36. John Locke, *Miscellaneous Papers*. In Lord Peter King, *The Life of John Locke with Extracts from His Correspondence, Journals, and Common-Place Books*, 2 vols. (London: Henry Colburn and Richard Bentley, 1830), vol. 2, pp. 122 - 23.

37. *Ibid.*, p. 120.

38. *Ibid.*

39. *Ibid.*

40. *Ibid.*

41. *Ibid.*, p. 121.

42. *Journal* entry, 1678.

43. *Ibid.*

44. *Miscellaneous Papers, op. cit.*, p. 127.

45. *An Essay concerning Human Understanding*, bk. 2, chap. 20, secs. 7 - 13.

46. *Ibid.*, sec. 14.

47. *Ibid.*, chap. 28, sec. 5.

48. *Ibid.*, sec. 7.

49. *Ibid.*, bk. 4, chap. 19, sec. 4.

50. *Ibid.*, bk. 2, chap. 28, sec. 9.

51. *Ibid.*, sec. 10.

52. Locke to Molyneux, March 30, 1696. Included in the eighth volume of the twelfth edition of *The Works of John Locke* (London, 1824).

53. *Journal* entry, February 8, 1677.

Chapter Three

1. Locke's dictum concerning the fundamental aim of education was derived from the ancient satirist Juvenal (first century A.D.) who described Roman society as hopelessly evil and advised men that they should pray only for the same goal of sanity and health.

2. Locke to Clarke, July 19, 1684.

3. *Ibid.*

4. *Ibid.*

5. *Ibid.*

6. René Descartes, *Meditations on the First Philosophy* (1644), Meditation 3.

7. René Descartes, *The Principles of Philosophy*, (1644), pt. 1, sec. 49.

8. Descartes, *Meditations*, Meditation 2.

9. *Ibid.*

10. *An Essay concerning Human Understanding*, bk. 2, chap. 1, sec. 2.

11. Locke to Clarke, July 19, 1684.

12. *An Essay concerning Human Understanding*, bk. 1, chap. 1, sec. 2.

13. *Ibid.*, sec. 3.

14. *Ibid.*, bk. 4, chap. 19, sec. 4.

15. *Ibid.*, bk. 1, chap. 1, sec. 5.

16. See S. S. Laurie, *Studies in the History of Educational Opinion from the Renaissance* (Cambridge: Cambridge University Press, 1903), especially the three chapters on Locke.

17. *An Essay concerning Human Understanding*, bk. 1, chap. 2, sec. 1.

18. *Ibid.*, sec. 3.

19. *Ibid.*, sec. 5.

20. *Ibid.*

21. *Ibid.*, sec. 9.

22. *Ibid.*, chap. 3, sec. 2.

23. *Ibid.*, sec. 8.

24. *Ibid.*, chap. 4, sec. 23.

25. Gottfried Wilhelm Leibniz, *New Essays concerning Human Understanding* (New York: Macmillan, 1896), pp. 16, 38.

26. *Ibid.*, preface.

27. *Ibid.*

28. *Ibid.*

29. *Ibid.*

30. John Dewey, *Leibniz's New Essays concerning Human Understanding* (Chicago: S. C. Griggs, 1888). Reprinted in *The Early Works of John Dewey: 1882 - 1898* (Carbondale, Illinois: Southern Illinois University Press, 1969), vol. 1, pp. 311-12.

31. Leibniz, *New Essays*, bk. 1, chap. 1, sec. 25.

32. *Ibid.*, bk. 2, chap. 1, sec. 2.

Chapter Four

1. Locke to Clarke, July 19, 1684. Published in Benjamin Rand, *The Correspondence of John Locke and Edward Clarke* (Cambridge Mass.: Harvard University Press, 1927) and reprinted in James L. Axtell, *The Educational Writings of John Locke: A Critical Edition with Introduction and Notes* (Cambridge: Cambridge University Press, 1968).

2 - 8. *Ibid.*

9 - 20. Quotations from letter of Locke to Clarke, September 1, 1685.

21 - 41. Quotations from letters of Locke to Clarke, February 8 - March 15, 1686.

42. Locke to Clarke, March 15, 1686.

43 - 66. Quotations from letter of Locke to Clarke, April 29, 1687.

67 - 73. Quotations from letter of Locke to Clarke, July 15, 1687.

74. Locke to Clarke, February 6, 1688.

75. *Ibid.*

76. Locke to Clarke, January 28, 1688 [- 9].

Chapter Five

1. A number of the terms employed by Locke have undergone evolutionary change over the years, "crazy" being one of them. Sick or frail was its meaning for Locke.

2. *Some Thoughts Concerning Education*, (1693) sec. 1.

3. *Ibid.* sec. 2.

4. *Ibid.*, sec. 3.

5. *Ibid.*, sec. 5.

6. *Ibid.*, sec. 10.

7. *Ibid.*, sec. 14.

8. *Ibid.*, sec. 18.

9. *Ibid.*, sec. 22.

10. *Ibid.*, sec. 21.

11. *Ibid.*, sec. 33.

12. *Ibid.*, sec. 36.

13. *Ibid.*, sec. 42.

14. *Ibid.*, sec. 43.

15. *Ibid.*, scc. 46.

16. *Ibid.*, sec. 49.

17. *Ibid.*, sec. 51.

18. *Ibid.*, sec. 52.

19. *Ibid.*, sec. 54.

20. *Ibid.*, sec. 55.

21. *Ibid.*, sec. 56.

22. *Ibid.*, sec. 64.

23. *Ibid.*, sec. 66.

24. *Ibid.*, sec. 71.

25. *Ibid.*, sec. 93.

26. *Ibid.*

27. *Ibid.*, sec. 94.

28. *Ibid.*

29. *Ibid.*, sec. 94.

30. *Ibid.*

31. *Ibid.*

32. *Ibid.*, sec. 95.

33. *Ibid.*, sec. 97.

34. *Ibid.*, sec. 98.

35. *Ibid.*

36. *Ibid.*, sec. 100.

37. *Ibid.*

38. *Ibid.*, sec. 108.

39. *Ibid.*, sec. 110.

40. *Ibid.*, sec. 115.

41. *Ibid.*

42. *Ibid.*

43. *Ibid.*
44. *Ibid.*
45. *Ibid.*
46. *Ibid.*, sec. 117.
47. *Ibid.*, sec. 131.
48. *Ibid.*, sec. 132.
49. *Ibid.*
50. *Ibid.*, sec. 135.
51. *Ibid.*, sec. 139.
52. *Ibid.*
53. *Ibid.*, sec. 141.
54. *Ibid.*, sec. 143.
55. Letters from Locke to Clarke, February 8 - March 15, 1686.
56. *Ibid.*
57. *Some Thoughts concerning Education*, sec. 149.

Chapter Six
1. Lord Peter King, *The Life of John Locke with Extracts from His Correspondence, Journals, and Common-Place Books*, 2 vols. (London: Henry Colburn and Richard Bentley, 1830), vol. 1, pp. 171 - 203.
2. James L. Axtell, *The Educational Writings of John Locke* (Cambridge: Cambridge University Press, 1968), pp. 405 - 22.
3. *Study*, vol. 1, p. 171.
4. *Ibid.*, pp. 171 - 72.
5. *Ibid.*, p. 173.
6. *Ibid.*, p. 174.
7. *Ibid.*, p. 176.
8. *Ibid.*, p. 177.
9. *Ibid.*, p. 179.
10. *Ibid.*, pp. 180 - 81.
11. *Ibid.*, p. 181.
12. *Ibid.*, p. 184.
13. *Ibid.*, p. 194.
14. *Ibid.*, p. 199.
15. *Ibid.*
16. John Locke, *Some Thoughts concerning Reading and Study for a Gentleman*, in vol. 2 of *The Works of John Locke* (London, 1824), p. 405.
17. *Ibid.*
18. *Ibid.*
19. *Ibid.*
20. *Ibid.*
21. *An Essay concerning Human Understanding*, bk. 1, chap. 1, sec. 8.
22. *Some Thoughts concerning Reading and Study for a Gentleman*, p. 406.
23. *Ibid.*

24. *Ibid.*

25. *Ibid.*

26. *Ibid.*, p. 407.

27. *Ibid.*, p. 411.

28. *Ibid.*

29. John Locke, "Draft Letter to the Countess of Peterborough," in *The Educational Writings of John Locke*, p. 393.

30. *Ibid.*

31. *Ibid.*, p. 395.

32. *Ibid.*, p. 396.

33. Locke to Molyneux, April 10, 1697.

34. Editor (probably Lord Peter King), "Advertisement to the Reader," in *Posthumous Works of Mr. Locke* (1706).

35. H. R. Fox-Bourne, *The Life of John Locke*, vol. 2, p. 443.

36. Thomas Fowler, Introduction to *Locke's Conduct of the Understanding* (Oxford: Clarendon Press, 1882), p. xxi.

37. *Ibid.*, p. xxiii.

38. See William Boyd, *From Locke to Montessori* (New York: Henry Holt, 1914); also his *The History of Western Education* (London: A. & A. Black, 1921).

39. John Locke, *Of the Conduct of the Understanding*, sec. 1.

40. *Ibid.*

41. *Ibid.*, sec. 3.

42. *Ibid.*

43. *Ibid.*, sec. 7.

44. E. L. Thorndike and R. S. Woodworth, "The Influence of Improvement in One Mental Function upon the Efficiency of Other Functions," *Psychological Review* 8 (1901), 147 - 261, 384 - 95, 553 - 64.

45. *Of the Conduct of the Understanding*, rev. ed., sec. 5.

46. Edwin R. Guthrie, *The Psychology of Learning,* (New York: Harper, 1952), p. 23.

47. *Ibid.*, p. 132.

48. *Of the Conduct of the Understanding*, sec. 4.

49. E. L. Thorndike, *Animal Intelligence: Experimental Studies* (New York: Macmillan, 1911), p. 244.

50. *Of the Conduct of the Understanding*, sec. 4.

51. *Ibid.*, sec. 19.

52. *Ibid.*, sec. 20.

53. *Ibid.*

54. *Ibid.*, sec. 14.

55. *Ibid.*, sec. 11.

56. *Ibid.*, sec. 10.

57. *Ibid.*, sec. 9.

58. *Ibid.*, sec. 24.

59. *Ibid.*, sec. 23.

60. *Ibid.*
61. *Ibid.*, sec. 24.
62. *Ibid.*
63. *Ibid.*, sec. 42.

Chapter Seven

1. Richard I. Aaron, *John Locke*, 3rd ed. (Oxford: Clarendon Press, 1971), pp. 302 - 3.
2. Hans Aarsleff, "Some Observations on Recent Locke Scholarship," in *John Locke: Problems and Perspectives*, ed. John W. Yolton (Cambridge: Cambridge University Press, 1969), p. 270.
3. *Ibid.*, p. 263.
4. *Ibid.*, p. 268.
5. Rosalie Colie, "The Essayist in His *Essay*," in *John Locke: Problems and Perspectives*, p. 234.
6. *Ibid.*, p. 236.
7. F. W. Garforth, Editor's Introduction to *Some Thoughts concerning Education*, by John Locke (New York: Barron's Educational Series, 1964), p. 17.
8. *Ibid.*, p. 18.
9. Robert Ulich, *Three Thousand Years of Educational Wisdom* (Cambridge, Mass.: Harvard University Press, 1954), p. 355.
10. *Ibid.*
11. S. J. Curtis and M. E. A. Boultwood, *A Short History of Educational Ideas* (London: University Tutorial Press, 1973), p. 246.
12. Robert Hebert Quick, *Essays on Educational Reformers* (New York: D. Appleton, 1890), p. 222.
13. *Ibid.*, p. 227.
14. *Ibid.*, p. 230.
15. F. Andrew Brown, "On Education: John Locke, Christian Wolff, and the 'Moral Weeklies,'" *University of California Publications in Modern Philology* 36 (1952), 149 - 72.
16. *Ibid.*, p. 153.
17. Alfred Adler, *The Science of Living* (New York: Doubleday, 1969), p. 10.
18. John Watson, *Psychology from the Standpoint of a Behaviorist* (Philadelphia: Lippincott, 1919), p. 268.
19. *Ibid.*, p. 270.
20. John Dewey, *Experience and Education* (New York: Collier, 1963), pp. 19 - 20.
21. William Boyd, *The History of Western Education*, p. 294.
22. *Ibid.*
23. *Ibid.*
24. William Boyd, *From Locke to Montessori*, p. 21.

25. John W. Yolton, *John Locke and Education* (New York: Random House, 1971), p. 91.

26. *Some Thoughts concerning Education*, sec. 217.

27. *Ibid.*

28. John W. Yolton, *John Locke and Education*, p. 91.

29. *Ibid.*

30. *Ibid.*, pp. 91 - 92.

31. John W. Yolton, *John Locke and the Way of Ideas* (London: Oxford University Press, 1956), p. viii.

32. Norman Kemp Smith, *John Locke (1632 - 1704)* (Manchester: Manchester University Press, 1933), p. 19.

33. *Ibid.*

34. *Ibid.*

35. *Ibid.*

36. *Ibid.*

Selected Bibliography of Locke's Writings on Education

1677 *Of Study.* Remarks on the subject written in France and included in Locke's *Journal*

1684 - Letters to Clarke. Contains instructions for the education of Clarke's
1691 son; the advice given to Clarke became the basis of Locke's principal book on education, *Some Thoughts concerning Education.*

1690 *An Essay concerning Human Understanding.* Locke's classic treatise containing a systematic account of his philosophy, including ideas important for the understanding of his views on education.

1693 *Some Thoughts concerning Education.* Locke's major, systematic, and definitive work on education.

1697 Draft letter to the Countess of Peterborough. Advice on study for the Countess's son, John.

1703 *Some Thoughts concerning Reading and Study for a Gentleman.* Advice on study supplied to the thirty-six-year-old Roger Clavel.

1706 *Of the Conduct of the Understanding.* Initially intended as an additional chapter to Locke's classic *Essay,* but never appeared as part of it.

Selected Bibliography of
Secondary Sources

AARON, RICHARD I. *John Locke.* 3rd ed. Oxford: Clarendon Press, 1971. A
  fine, scholarly approach to the life and general works of Locke.
ADAMSON, JOHN W. *Pioneers of Modern Education in the Seventeenth
  Century.* New York: Teachers College Press, Columbia University,
  1971. Initially published as *Pioneers of Modern Education 1600-1700.*
  Cambridge: Cambridge University Press, 1905.
———. *The Educational Writings of John Locke.* New York: Longmans,
  Green, 1912. Contains selections from Locke's *Some Thoughts on
  Education* and *Conduct of the Understanding.*
AXTELL, JAMES L. *The Educational Writings of John Locke.* Cambridge:
  Cambridge University Press, 1968. Contains a biography of Locke, a
  commentary on his writings about education, and the texts of the
  following educational writings: *Some Thoughts concerning Education;*
  the important letters of Locke to Clarke; Locke's draft letter to the
  Countess of Peterborough; *Some Thoughts concerning Reading and
  Study for a Gentleman;* and *Of Study.*
BONNO, GABRIEL. "Lettres Inédites de Le Clerc à Locke." *University of
  California Publications in Modern Philology,* vol. 52 (1959). Le
  Clerc's letters edited with an introduction and notes by Bonno.
BOYD, WILLIAM. *From Locke to Montessori: A Critical Account of the
  Montessori Point of View.* New York: Henry Holt, 1914. Contains a
  chapter on Locke and a historical, critical account of the Montessori
  viewpoint.
———. *The History of Western Education.* London: A. & A. Black, 1921.
  Devotes a fair portion to Locke's educational theory.
BROWN, F. ANDREW. "On Education: John Locke, Christian Wolff, and the
  'Moral Weeklies,' " *University of California Publications in Modern
  Philology* 36 (1952), 149 - 72. Contains an evaluation of Locke's
  educational ideas and their important influence on German educational
  reform.
CRANSTON, MAURICE. *John Locke: A Biography.* New York: Macmillan,
  1957. Finest of the recent biographies; also contains a portrait of Locke
  in 1685 by Sylvanus Brownover.

CURTIS, S. J., AND BOULTWOOD, M. E. A. *A Short History of Educational Ideas.* London: University Tutorial Press, 1953. A fine history with a chapter devoted to Locke.

DUNN, JOHN. *The Political Thought of John Locke.* Cambridge: Cambridge University Press, 1969. A historical account of the argument of the *Two Treatises of Government.* Helpful since Locke makes much of an education in politics.

FOWLER, THOMAS. *Locke.* London: Macmillan, 1880. A two-hundred-page biography of Locke.

————. *Locke's Conduct of the Understanding.* Oxford: Clarendon Press, 1882. Contains the *Conduct* in its entirety together with a biographical introduction.

FOX-BOURNE, H. R. *The Life of John Locke.* 2 vols. New York: Harper, 1876. An early classic biography containing a variety of primary material.

GARFORTH, F. W. *John Locke: Some Thoughts concerning Education.* Woodbury, N. Y.: Barron's Educational Series, 1964. In addition to the *Some Thoughts* there is a brief selection from *Of the Conduct of the Understanding* plus a valuable but brief glossary of terms used by Locke which have undergone a change in meaning; also provided are an introduction and commentary.

GAY, PETER. *John Locke on Education.* New York: Bureau of Publications, Teachers College, Columbia University, 1964. An introduction is supplied in addition to Locke's *Some Thoughts concerning Education.*

GIBSON, JAMES. *Locke's Theory of Knowledge and Its Historical Relations.* Cambridge: Cambridge University Press, 1917.

HARGREAVES-MAWDSLEY, W. N. *Oxford in the Age of John Locke.* Norman, Oklahoma: University of Oklahoma Press, 1973. Contains an introduction in addition to the text of *Some Thoughts concerning Education.*

HARRISON, JOHN, AND LASLETT, PETER. *The Library of John Locke.* 2nd ed. Oxford: Clarendon Press, 1971. Contains a discussion of Locke and his books, including the development of his library, composition of the final collection, Locke's library practice, master catalogue, and the man as book collector.

HOFSTADTER, ALBERT. *Locke and Scepticism.* Ph.D. dissertation, Columbia University, 1935. Ann Arbor, Michigan: University Microfilms, 1970.

KING, LORD PETER. *The Life of John Locke, with Extracts from his Correspondence, Journals, and Common-Place Books.* 2 vols. London: Henry Colburn and Richard Bentley, 1830.

KRAUS, JOHN L. *John Locke: Empiricist, Atomist, Conceptualist, and Agnostic.* New York: Philosophical Library, 1968. An examination of Locke's theory of universal ideas and their relation to the science of physical things.

LAMPRECHT, STERLING POWER. *The Moral and Political Philosophy of John Locke.* New York: Columbia University Press, 1918. A scholarly and systematic examination of Locke's philosophy.

LASLETT, PETER. *John Locke: Two Treatises of Government.* 2nd ed.

Cambridge: Cambridge University Press, 1967. A critical edition with an introduction and critical apparatus.

LAURIE, S. S. *Studies in the History of Educational Opinion from the Renaissance.* New York: Augustus M. Kelley Publishers, 1969. Originally published in 1903 by Cambridge University Press.

LE CLERC, JEAN. *The Life and Character of Mr. John Locke. Bibliothèque Choise,* VI, 5. Translated from the French by T. F. P. Gent, and included in *Locke's Essay concerning Human Understanding,* ed. Mary Whiton Calkins, 2nd ed., Chicago: Open Court, 1912.

LEIBNIZ, GOTTFRIED WILHELM. *New Essays concerning Human Understanding.* New York: Macmillan, 1896. Excellent rebuttal of Locke's attack on innate ideas from the standpoint of continental rationalism.

LEYDEN, W. VON *John Locke: Essays on the Law of Nature: The Latin Text with a Translation, Introduction and Notes, Together with Transcripts of Locke's Shorthand in his Journal for 1676.* Oxford: Clarendon Press, 1954. This edited work contains an almost one-hundred-page scholarly introduction and draws on the Lovelace Collection at the Bodleian Library, Oxford University.

LODGE, EDMUND. *Portraits of Illustrious Personages of Great Britain: With Biographical and Historical Memoirs of Their Lives and Actions.* 12 vols. Boston: Dana Estes, 1902. Volume 9 contains a portrait of John Locke engraved by H. Robinson from the original painting by Sir Godfrey Kneller that is in the collection at Christ Church, Oxford University; also contains Locke's biography.

LOUGH, JOHN. *Locke's Travels in France 1675 - 1679: As Related in his Journals, Correspondence and Other Papers.* Cambridge: Cambridge University Press, 1953. An account of Locke's four years in France, together with an introduction and notes by the editor; also contains a portrait of Locke (c. 1675) by John Greenhill.

MABBOTT, J. D. *John Locke.* London: Macmillan, 1973. Purports to view Locke as a philosopher in perspective, examining his arguments in the light of recent scholarly contributions.

MACLEAN, KENNETH. *John Locke and English Literature of the Eighteenth Century.* New Haven: Yale University Press, 1936. Reissued, New York: Russell & Russell, 1962. A critical study of Locke as criticized, popularized, and adapted by English literature of the eighteenth century.

MORRIS, C. R. *Locke, Berkeley, Hume.* Oxford: Clarendon Press, 1931. Contains a biography of Locke in addition to a discussion of his epistemological, moral, and political theories.

O'CONNOR, D. J. *John Locke.* Melbourne: Penguin Books, 1952.

OGILVIE, R. M. *Latin and Greek: A History of the Influence of the classics on English Life from 1600 to 1800.* Hamden, Conn: Archon Books, 1964.

OGILVIE, VIVIAN. *The English Public School.* London: B. T. Bradford, 1957.

OSLER, WILLIAM. *An Alabama Student and Other Biographical Essays.* Oxford: Oxford University Press, 1908. Contains a chapter on the biography of Locke as a physician.

QUICK, ROBERT HEBERT. *Essays on Educational Reformers.* Cincinnati: Robert Clarke, 1883; rev. ed., New York: D. Appleton, 1890. The first edition offers a better account of Lockean educational theory.

QUICK, ROBERT HEBERT. Introduction and Notes to *Some Thoughts concerning Education,* by John Locke. Rev. ed. Cambridge: Cambridge University Press, 1884. Contains over ninety pages of biography and critical notes; also Locke's essay *of Study.*

RAND, BENJAMIN. *The Correspondence of John Locke and Edward Clarke.* Cambridge, Mass.: Harvard University Press, 1927. Also contains a biographical study.

SELIGER, MARTIN. *The Liberal Politics of John Locke.* London: Allen and Unwin, 1968; reprinted, New York: Frederick A Praeger, 1969.

SMITH, J. W. ASHLEY. *The Birth of Modern Education: The Contribution of the Dissenting Academies, 1660 - 1800.* London: Independent Press, 1954.

SMITH, NORMAN KEMP. *John Locke (1632 - 1704).* Manchester: Manchester University Press, 1933. The Adamson Lecture for 1932.

TAGART, EDWARD. *Locke's Writings and Philosophy Historically Considered, and Vindicated from the Charge of Contributing to the Scepticism of Hume.* London: Longmans, Brown, Green, and Longmans, 1855.

ULICH, ROBERT. *Three Thousand Years of Educational Wisdom.* 2nd ed. Cambridge, Mass.: Harvard University Press, 1954. Includes Locke.

WEBB, THOMAS E. *The Intellectualism of Locke: An Essay.* London: Longman, Brown, Green, Longmans, and Roberts, 1857. Purports to prove that Locke is an intellectualist rather than an empiricist or sensationalist.

WOOLHOUSE, R. S. *Locke's Philosophy of Science and Knowledge.* New York: Barnes & Noble, 1971. Deals with Locke's theory of natural and scientific laws and our knowledge of them.

YOLTON, JOHN W., ed., *John Locke: An Essay concerning Human Understanding.* London: J. M. Dent, 1961. Locke's *Essay* edited with an introduction by the editor.

———. *John Locke: Problems and Perspectives.* Cambridge: Cambridge University Press, 1969. Collection of essays by Lockean scholars.

———. *John Locke and Education.* New York: Random House, 1971. One of the Studies in the Western Educational Tradition series.

———. *John Locke and the Way of Ideas.* London: Oxford University Press, 1956; reprinted 1968.

———. *Locke and the Compass of Human Understanding.* Cambridge: Cambridge University Press, 1970. A selective commentary on Locke's *Essay.*

Index